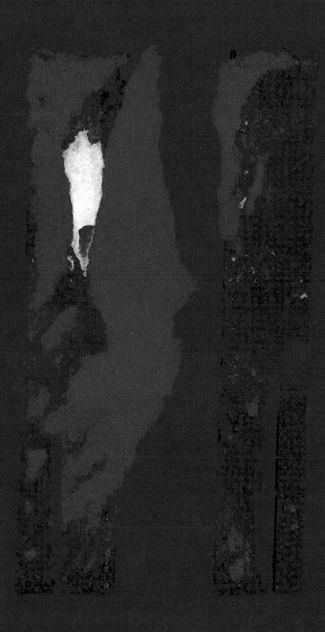

Garth
Brooks

Garth Brooks

The Road out of Santa Fe

By Matt O'Meilia

University of Oklahoma Press : Norman and London

SONG CREDITS

"1982" © 1985 Songs of Grand Coalition/Southern Grand Alliance. International copyright secured. All rights reserved. Used by permission. "Drinkin' My Baby Goodbye" © 1984 Cabin Fever Music. Writer: Charlie Daniels. All rights reserved. Used by permission. "Luck of the Draw" © 1986 Golden Ladder Music, Inc., and Silver Cradle Music, Inc. Writers: Bob Childers, Greg Jacobs, and Garth Brooks. All rights reserved. Used by permission.

Library of Congress Cataloging-in-Publication Data

O'Meilia, Matt, 1962–
    Garth Brooks: the road out of Santa Fe / by Matt O'Meilia.
      p.   cm.
    ISBN 0–8061–2907–7 (alk. paper)
    1. Brooks, Garth. 2. Santa Fe (Musical group). 3. Singers—United States—Biography. 4. Country musicians—United States—Biography. 5. Country music—Oklahoma—History and criticism. I. Title.
ML420.B7796045   1997
782.42′1642′092—dc20   96–42095
[B]   CIP

Text design by Debora Hackworth.

1 2 3 4 5 6 7 8 10

For Meg, my favorite cowgirl

Distinction is the consequence, never the object, of a great mind.

—Author unknown

Contents

ILLUSTRATIONS

ILLUSTRATIONS

Author's Note

I would like to acknowledge that at no time in my career with Santa Fe did I carry a tape recorder. I am compelled to state this because some may wonder how I could have remembered all of the dialogue contained herein. Much of it I do remember. Much of it was remembered for me; I thoroughly picked the brains of my former band members—except Garth—and the various other people I've included in the story.

I tried to interview Garth. Oh *boy*, how I tried. I did everything but parachute into his backyard. As I completed sections of the book, I routinely sent them to his home and requested his comments. I left messages on his personal answering machine. I petitioned him through mutual friends. One of those friends relayed this message back: "Tell O'Meilia I've received everything he sent, but I can't write him back." His saying "can't" instead of "won't" led me to suspect that he is by contract forbidden to enter into any venture, even indirectly, without permission from one of his handlers.

So, I wrote the book without Garth. After I finished, I was glad I never did talk to him because his noninvolvement helped me portray him more objectively, even though the style of my book is inherently subjective.

Deciding on a style to present the material was not easy. I began by writing about all the characters, including myself, in the third person. But I abandoned that idea because the book started sounding like a newspaper article, and I was not comfortable extending an impersonal, journalistic style for the length of a book. In the end, what I decided felt most natural was a kind of hybrid style, the novelistic memoir.

The story's dialogue is of three varieties: that which is verbatim, that which is paraphrased, and that which is created using literary license. The dialogue that occurs in scenes when I was not present is gleaned from my interviews with people who were. Fabricated dialogue, which is extremely minimal, is for the purpose of reconstructing the chronology of events and occasionally to help smooth a transition between anecdotes.

Acknowledgments

Many thanks to those who traveled with me on the long and treacherous road to authorship: Cathy Balch, Terry Balch, Rick Belatti at *Stillwater NewsPress*, Bob Brown at Oklahoma State University Edmon Low Library, Stephanie Brown, Margaret and Ron Butler, Bob Childers, Jennifer Cobb at the *Tulsa World*, Paul House, Mike Hufford, Kevin Maloney, Matt McNearney, Mac and Millie Overholt, Bob Reeder, Randy Ramer, Dale "Raddler" Shipley, Jana Shipley, Edmund D. "Bink" Simank, Sr., Dean Sims, Buddy Watson, Adam Scott Weintraub, and John Wooley at the *Tulsa World*.

Special thanks to my two amiable, cooperative, non-money-hungry friends in Nashville: Betty Jo Fowler (Cabin Fever Music) and Pat Halverson (Songs of Grand Coalition/Southern Grand Alliance).

Very special thanks to John Drayton, Alice Stanton, and everyone at University of Oklahoma Press, Sally

ACKNOWLEDGMENTS

Antrobus, Dorothy and Tom Egan, Charlie Jennemann, Gordon Weaver, Jay and Jody O'Meilia, Andrew and Madeline for bearing with their overbearing daddy, and my wife, Kim, who raised this project from the dead.

And to Garth and Sandy, Tom and Jeri, Mike, Craig, Jed, Dale, and Troy, this book is my thanks to you for being part of my life.

xvi

Garth
Brooks

INTRODUCTION

Driving back from the Bamboo Ballroom in Enid, Oklahoma, one early Sunday morning, Garth and I were musing about fame and fortune. Idle talk, I thought, until Garth blurted out, "I want to be . . . America's Band!" Even through the gloom of the car interior I could see his eyes burning with intensity.

I barely kept from laughing. *America's Band?* Sometimes Garth was a walking, talking stalk of pure corn. After all, if there were such a thing as America's Band, who would it be? In 1986, Garth would have bestowed the crown upon Bob Seger and the Silver Bullet Band, which he then considered the quintessential American rock 'n roll group. At least once a gig, and usually twice, we did "Old Time Rock 'n Roll," "Night Moves," "Horizontal Bop," and other Seger stuff, along with our nightly homages to Georges Jones and Strait.

Maybe Garth still thinks Seger's the king of rock and

the Georges the head honchos of country. But it doesn't matter what he thinks anymore. He's now a member of the band that, for millions of fans, dwarfs all others. Ladies and gentlemen, America's Band: *Garth Brooks and Stillwater*.

Before he reached near-mythological status, though, he and I were part of the band Santa Fe. From March 1986 through January 1987, I was Santa Fe's drummer. We played mostly in Stillwater, Oklahoma, home of the Oklahoma State University Cowboys. We were the house band for one of Stillwater's strangest bars. And from the first time we ever played together, we were good. Real good, as a matter of fact. How can I be so sure? For one thing, Garth could sing then like he does now. Then there were Tom and Mike Skinner, who could harmonize as soulfully as the Everly brothers, and Jed Lindsey, who could strangle a guitar without mercy.

4

Soon we got much better, good enough to open for two established acts, the New Grass Revival and Johnny Paycheck, as well as a camera-shy young neo-hillbilly named Dwight Yoakam, who had just put out his first album. We also performed twice on *A.M. Oklahoma*, an Oklahoma City morning television show. And that was just within the first few months of playing together. For five local yokels who had just gotten started, we were doing as well as any of us could hope. Except Garth. These were small accomplishments in his incandescent eyes, stepping stones to an implausibly successful career, one that deep, deep down in his heart he knew would occur. I say *knew* because I believe all wildly famous people are not only destined to be so but also receive a vision of the future at some point in their lives. Some keep it a secret, or simply cannot articulate it, and plod right along, taking the correct turns at each fork in the road, hand in hand with Serendipity all the way to the summit. For others, like Garth, destiny burns through their being. Garth used to tell people he'd be big. They'd laugh, of course, but not because they thought he lacked talent or sincerity. For most normal, eight-to-five folk, fame is simply alien to reality.

On the surface, there's no great secret to Garth's fame. He is a driven man. Everything he has accomplished he wanted badly. He worked hard. I've never known anyone in any walk of life who was so completely hell-bent on making it to the top. That's why few who know him were surprised Garth entered the spotlight. But when his fame spilled over into the realm of cultural phenomenon, everyone—including Garth—dropped their jaws in disbelief.

But this book is about a famous person before he became famous. It's about a better-than-average but not necessarily spectacular band called Santa Fe, which existed for a little more than a year. It's about the places we played, the people we met, and the events that foreshadowed a legendary musical career. This isn't a book about how I knew Garth better than anyone else. In many ways I never knew him. I certainly never understood his passionate nature. Sometimes he was like an actor in a bad melodrama, like the time he told me about wanting Santa Fe to be "America's Band." I was sure he was putting me on. I guess he wasn't.

Now that he's caught up with his sublime future sooner than anyone expected, Garth probably is wondering what's left for him to achieve. That's another book. For now, let's go back about ten years and lend this legend a little humanity. Garth needs it. I know he'd agree.

1

SETTING THE STAGE

Wednesday night in Stillwater, Oklahoma, spring 1985. Small groups of young men and women cruise up and down a four-block strip along Washington Street between University and Sixth, known to the faithful simply as the Strip. They laugh loudly. They whoop and holler. They shout salutations to friends they spot sprawled on the fraternity lawn across the street and trade good-natured invectives. The school year is drawing to a close, and some of the revelers have just begun one of the many pre-graduation parties that will bring their academic careers to a blurry close.

Overlooking this scene some three hundred yards straight north is Oklahoma State University's Edmon Low Library. As usual, the mechanical engineering students and postgrads are there. A few business and education majors are hiding in the corners, writing letters home, napping, slurping a contraband soft drink, even studying. Edmon Low is not nearly as lonely as it was when eighteen-year-olds could legally buy all the beer their parents could afford. But in 1983, when the State of Oklahoma made the magic age twenty-one, the library began an era of unprecedented activity while the gloriously infamous Strip began to die.

Still, the students prowl, but not in the shoulder-to-shoulder traffic of the Strip's heyday. Some stop in at the Coney Island for a beer and a game of pool. A brave few wander down to the southern edge of the Strip, to dark, smoky, graffiti-plastered Nuevo Wavo, where a garage band is playing painfully loud Byrds and Doors songs. Decked-out sorority sisters file into the Turning Point for Ladies' Night and nonstop Prince dance mixes. Awkward freshman boys are making copies at Kinko's and having fantasy upon fantasy about every tanned, long-legged coed who jiggles in.

Meanwhile, twenty-three-year-old Troyal Garth Brooks is setting up his Peavey mini-PA system at Willie's Wild West Saloon, located smack dab in the middle of the Strip. A few of the regulars bang through Willie's swinging doors. Garth is swiftly plugging in wires, turning knobs, tapping the mike, a routine he's performed countless times. "Check, one, two."

A nervous girl of about nineteen approaches Garth. "Do you know any Jimmy Buffet?" She's obviously not a regular.

"Yes, ma'am," he replies while adjusting his microphone stand. "Which one?"

"I love 'Come Monday.' "

"So do I. I'll do that one first set."

She looks back at her giggling friends. "Just ask him,"

Running around nude was popular during the Strip's heyday in the 1970s. Streaker Night was an annual event for many years, occurring the Thursday before OSU's spring break, until the police decided the students were having too much fun and banned the practice. After nudity was banned, the legal drinking age was raised. Students figured out that they could get naked and drink elsewhere, so the Strip began to dry up. Photo credit: *Stillwater NewsPress*.

one shouts.

"Oh, all right," she says. "Do you know that dirty David Allan Coe song?"

"Which one?" says Garth, patiently indulging her while strapping on his Ovation guitar.

"Oh, I don't know what it's called," the embarrassed girl says. "I really don't want to hear it anyway. You know some James Taylor, don't you?"

"I'm gonna do one right now."

She returns to her table. Garth fingers his guitar and sends "Fire and Rain" out to the group of anxious, underage girls who have come to Willie's to relax a little before studying for tomorrow's test. Four hours, five pitchers, and two packs of cigarettes later, the girls decide it's time to go. They go straight to bed and wake up ten minutes before class with horrible hangovers. They throw on their sweats and run to class, trying not to vomit on the way. They flunk their test, of course, but there's one consolation: they are now members of the informal Garth Brooks fan club.

For two years, members of the club planted themselves in Willie's every Wednesday night to hear Garth play. He had a very good voice, a rare commodity for a local entertainer. He could pick a guitar pretty well, too. He made it look easy. So easy, in fact, that after a few beers, the Willie's patrons came to believe singing was their calling in life. Toward the end of the evening, Garth had everyone—the loud, lewd frat boys; the burly pool shooters; the locals who arrived at six and never relinquished their bar stools; the tight-jeaned, snuff-dipping Ag majors in ropers and stiffly starched work shirts; the shuffleboard freaks; the waitresses, bartenders, and even old Wild Willie himself— singing along to "American Pie," one of Garth's hallmark covers.

Most bar singers in Stillwater were background music, but Garth was there to perform, not to be white noise. He performed even if he didn't want to be there, even if he was so sick of playing at Willie's he wanted to puke, and even if there were only three people in the bar who couldn't care less how good he was. Adoring crowds were icing on the cake, he reasoned. He smiled. He flirted with the girls. He joked around and made everyone feel at home. He gave a professional show no matter what. He was convinced

Garth at Willie's, 1985. Willie's is located in the middle of Stillwater's popular Strip. Garth's regular Wednesday night gig helped him hone his musical skills and expand his repertoire. Photo by Jana Shipley.

that every performance would make him a little bit better, bring him one step closer to his goal. Willie's was where he honed his talents, paid his dues. It was his practice hall and his practice audience. Someday it would all pay off. He didn't know exactly how, but it *had* to. Someone as good as Garth stuck in Willie's for the rest of his life? Why, that would be the highest injustice. Sure, a lot of musicians more talented than Garth had been singing their hearts out a lot longer without getting their big break. But he couldn't get caught up in other people's reality. No matter how good you are, you can't wait for big things to happen. Garth's marketing classes had burned one tenet into his mind: reality is what you create it to be.

So, after many months of playing at Willie's and at friends' wedding receptions and parties, he was ready. Everyone loved him in Stillwater. Why wouldn't they love him just as much in Nashville? Sure, he'd have to work hard and everything, but he was used to that. The time had come. Everyone told him he should give it a shot, that he'd make it for sure. Garth didn't need anyone to tell him that. He knew. The fan club knew. So did his family back in Yukon, Oklahoma. He quit his job at the sporting goods store and announced that he was off to pursue his dream. It wasn't easy to leave because he truly never expected to see anyone in Stillwater ever again, including his girlfriend, Sandy Mahl. But, he told himself, a man's got to follow his heart, the price of fame is dear, and all that jazz.

In the summer of 1985, while most new college grads were back home mowing lawns and driving ice-cream trucks in between job interviews, Garth Brooks hit the happy trail to Tennessee and glory, playing his James Taylor and Chris LeDoux tapes all the way, singing along, dreaming, occasionally getting nervous but then quickly reassuring himself, buoyed by pride that finally he had the maturity and the confidence to take such a huge step.

2

ROUNDUP

You'd have to spend a lifetime of research in Edmon Low to find a world-renowned human being who didn't suffer at least one large setback before reaching his goal. Great businessmen, athletes, entertainers, religious leaders—they've all turned pain into fuel for their fire.

Driving nonstop from Stillwater, Garth pulled off I-40 into Nashville and went straight to the office of Merlin Littlefield, vice president of ASCAP, the giant music publishing company, to learn a little about the business and begin the nauseating process of making connections. A mutual friend from the OSU Posse Club—a civic-affairs organization made up of students, alumni, and administrators—had set up the meeting. Garth walked past the country music memorabilia on the walls, entered a big reception area, and walked up to a secretary.

"Howdy, ma'am," he said, trying to keep his nerves

under control, "I'm Garth Brooks, here to see Mr. Littlefield."

"He'll be right with you, Mr. Brooks," she said. "You can have a seat. Would you like some coffee?"

"No, thanks, ma'am. I'm nervous enough as it is." Garth fiddled with the demo tape he'd recorded in Stillwater, turning it over and over in his sweaty hands. Littlefield's door opened and Garth stood up.

"I'm Garth Brooks, Mr. Littlefield," he said, extending his hand. "Pleasure to meet you." Littlefield eyed Garth's tape. "Let's hear what you got, son."

Garth followed Merlin Littlefield into the office and sat down in the chair in front of the big mahogany desk. Littlefield put in the tape and listened, poker-faced like any music industry executive. After the tape stopped, Littlefield turned to Garth without a change of expression and gave him the lowdown on the Nashville scene.

16

"Son, in this town, even if you're good you'll be lucky to make a living. I see guys like you all the time. Now, I think you've got a pretty good voice. Not bad at all. I've heard better and I've heard a lot worse. The funny thing is, guys worse than you can make it big and guys much better end up in the sewer. And another thing . . ."

On and on it went. Garth sat there like a kid getting a lecture from his father. He wasn't emotionally ready for this kind of reality. Instead of feeling the warm embrace of the music establishment, he felt as if he'd been caught breaking a window. In the middle of Littlefield's diatribe, a man barged in.

"Excuse me, Merlin. Sorry to interrupt, but I need to ask you something."

Littlefield introduced the man to Garth; he turned out

to be a songwriter Garth had heard of, someone who had written a few hits. Garth was impressed, but only momentarily.

"Merlin," he said, sounding rather desperate, "I need five hundred bucks. To pay off a loan."

Garth nearly laid an egg. Here was a guy who'd written stuff that actually made it onto an album, and he needed a measly five hundred bucks. "Shoot, man," Garth laughed, "I made that much money in a week playing back in Oklahoma."

Merlin and the songwriter looked at Garth as if he had two heads. "Then I suggest," said the experienced but destitute scribe, "that you go back."

The visit with Merlin worked its magic on Garth. That night he sat in his hotel room and stared at the ceiling. He suddenly felt an acute homesickness, one that overpowered everything, even his greatest fear: returning to Oklahoma to face the worst humiliation of his life. Disillusioned and disheartened, he left the very next morning. James Taylor and Chris LeDoux could not comfort him. He did not speak nor sing nor drum on the steering wheel. He listened to nothing but the whirr of his wheels on the highway home—to his real home in Yukon, where he could hide from the snickering and finger-pointing that surely awaited him in Stillwater. His mother, Colleen, a Capitol recording artist in the 1950s, offered her son all the consolation, empathy, and encouragement he could wallow in. It was the most miserable period of his life.

17

But soon he got fed up with living like an escaped convict and decided to return to Stillwater to face the music. He then discovered what true friendship is all about, as everyone welcomed him with open arms. Sandy required

The interior of Willie's. Willie's was where it all began for Garth. Photo by the author.

18   a little extra groveling, but it didn't take long before they were once again the happy pair. He even got his old job back at DuPree Sports. No one razzed him or told him he was a big loser—not to his face, anyway. When Garth returned to the microstage at Willie's, the Wednesday night club greeted him like a war hero. But as he resumed playing those same old songs and watching those same old faces inhaling suds and cig after cig after cig, he sensed his Nashville dream evaporating in the warmth and security of local-hero status. So, right there on the smallest stage in the world, Garth devised a plan to sever his umbilical cord from Willie's and return to Nashville. Next time, though, he wouldn't be alone.

I got to know Garth by dropping by DuPree Sports nearly

every day to visit my girlfriend, Suzi, who worked there as a T-shirt designer. Everyone seemed to know Garth, or at least know of him. He jabbered with anyone who walked into the store. He didn't sell a lot of merchandise, but no one cared. His bosses, Ed and Ann Watkins, were two of his biggest fans. Garth was one helluva singer, they said.

I had never seen Garth play. I was busy with my own band at the time, so I really didn't get out to see anyone else. Besides, I was a typical rock 'n roll snob. I rolled my eyes when people drooled about how great Garth was. Who wanted to listen to some hayseed sing "Your Cheatin' Heart" at that dump Willie's? Deep down, though, one of the main reasons I detested country music was that I was scared of the people who normally listened to it. Country music meant hard-ass rednecks in pickups who got drunk and beat the hell out of guys like me. I had run across my share of ruthless country types who drank fightin' liquor. You didn't have to look too far in Stillwater.

In March 1986, my rock band dissolved. At the time, I was finishing up my second degree, in philosophy, and working on the longest college career in history. Because the band was my only source of income, I made yet another trip to the parental well, asking my father if he would lend me enough money to finish the semester. He told me that his patience and his checkbook were both exhausted. It was the ultimatum I had dreaded but knew was inevitable. About a week after Dad cut my supply line, there was a knock at the front door. It was Garth. I stepped out on the front porch.

"Hey, man, I heard your band broke up."

For a country guy, Garth sure said 'man' a lot. "Yeah, it just didn't work out." My fear alarm suddenly went off as

19

The exterior of Willie's, with DuPree Sports in the background. Photo by the author.

20

I intuited the nature of his visit.

"You wanna be in a band?" he asked.

"You mean *country* music?" I gulped, unable to conceal my disdain.

"No, man, not straight country," he assured me. "I like everything. James Taylor, Lynyrd Skynyrd, Bob Seger, the Allman Brothers. People like that."

"Yeah, they're all right, I guess. But what kind of country stuff? Hank Williams?" Except for Roy Clark and some of the other regulars on *Hee Haw*, which my family used to watch on Saturdays during dinner for lack of anything better on, Hank was the only country singer who immediately came to mind.

"Well, I'm a big fan of George Jones," Garth said proudly. "And we'll probably do some Randy Travis and George Strait and Dwight Yoakam—some of the newer guys like that."

I didn't recognize one name. "Well, I don't know."

"We'll make two hundred a week. We'll be the house band at a club called Bink's."

I couldn't believe it. "Two hundred? Dollars? Each?"

"Yeah," Garth laughed. "Is that enough?"

My mind buzzed. That was more money than I'd ever made in my life. I could pay for school. I could eat something other than macaroni and cheese. But C&W? The dregs of music? I imagined myself in a cowboy hat, bolo tie, and a leather belt with my name on it, trying to beat my bass drum wearing cowboy boots. My mouth was forming the word "no" when I recalled the recent conversation with my father—the gnashing of his teeth and trembling of his voice.

"Let me think about it," I said.

21

"The other guys are coming over tomorrow night to talk about everything. You've heard of the Skinner Brothers, haven't you?"

I thought for a moment. "Have they ever been on *Hee Haw*?"

"No, man. Just come over at seven."

"Where do you live?"

Garth pointed to the duplex two doors away. "Right there. Think you can find it all right?"

I didn't know he lived so close. Man, I thought, I need to get out more often.

After he left, I started wondering why he asked *me* to play. I assumed he must have been pretty desperate to ask someone with such a serious lack of respect for country music. But he didn't know that. I didn't wear rock 'n roll like a badge of honor, with long hair and tattoos and leather and earrings and all of that gimmicky stuff. I never understood guys who felt it necessary to project such an affected, hell-raiser image all the time. Maybe they were afraid someone like Garth would ask them to play in a band.

It would seem that the promise of steady money and parental appeasement would make the decision to switch musical genres a no-brainer. A decision-maker like Garth certainly wouldn't have made a big dilemma out of it. When he first started playing Willie's, for example, he did nothing but 1970s easy-listening stuff—Dan Fogelberg and James Taylor and Don McLean. When someone suggested that he would get better overall crowd response by adding some country tunes to his repertoire, the next week he was doing George Strait and Merle Haggard songs as if he'd learned them in the crib. Garth and I were born only six days apart but he was by years my senior in understanding the necessity of being practical. I was a student, had never been anything but a student, and therefore was living in an abstract, idealistic world, a world of observation. My life was theory. In the development of my artistic consciousness—which began at age nine with a simultaneous discovery of rock and jazz—I had concluded, on the basis of hearing a few boring Conway Twitty songs, that C&W was a putrid form of music, listened to only by people with no taste whatsoever. I further believed that if I were actually to stoop to participate in creating such abysmally infantile noise, my circle of equally impractical friends would laugh at me and never talk to me again, thinking I'd completely lost my principles. But faced with the reality of starvation, suddenly I was forced to consider that which was once beneath my very being, something that compared in my juvenile mind to a Yankee going over to the Confederate side.

I lay in bed that night with such thoughts, such idealistic angst, and just when I'd decided that I'd rather operate a kissing booth at a leper colony than be in a country band, I remembered a chance encounter with my all-time musical hero a few months earlier. Buddy Rich had brought his band to Stillwater for a performance at OSU's Seretean Center. I couldn't believe my luck, couldn't get over the fact that the greatest musician in the world was going to be playing three blocks away from my house in Stillwater, Oklahoma. My friends and I scored perfect seats on the second row. We were running late for the show so we decided to take a shortcut through the back door of the auditorium. As soon as we opened the door, Buddy and his boys came out of their tour bus and walked in right behind us. I wheeled around and stuck my trembling, sweaty hand into his, the most efficient metacarpus God ever created. I imagined Buddy's power and control shooting into my fingertips. It was one of the most poignant moments of my life. My only wish is that my ability to talk hadn't suddenly abandoned me: "Duh . . . hope . . . you have . . . good show." Buddy smirked and mumbled something like, "Yeah, whatever you say, man."

We ran in and took our seats just as Buddy was leading his band onstage. He ambled over to his trap set with such ease of movement, such grace, acknowledging the thundering ovation with a wink, a wave, and a quick grin. He sat down and immediately counted his band into the first number. He was the coolest human being I'd ever seen in my life, so nonchalant with his total mastery of rhythm and syncopation. He literally tore the drums apart: the band had to stop during one song because the snares of his drum snapped under the pressure, like guitar strings coming unraveled. A technician ran in and began frantically repairing the drum while Buddy walked around the stage with a microphone, ad-libbing stories about where they'd been the night before. After the snare was fixed, Buddy resumed blowing our minds.

Nobody was in a class with Buddy Rich. He had ascended to such a musical threshold that it seemed he could simply will his hands and feet to do whatever he commanded, no matter how impossible or ridiculous it seemed. But there he was, touring around in a bus and stopping in the middle of Oklahoma, a guy who could be selling out Carnegie Hall every night of every year of every decade. That's when it occurred to me that despite his superhuman aura, he was fundamentally a working-class guy, a man who did what he had to do in order to make a living. He just happened to be one of the extraordinarily rare people who picked the profession nobody in the entire world could ever do better.

So the next night I made the forty-yard trek to Garth's place. I stepped up onto his creaky porch and heard guitar music. Garth was inside, flat-picking on his Ovation. The door was open, and he motioned me in with a nod. The first thing I noticed was the picture of John Wayne hung prominently behind his chair. His apartment was like most of the holes my friends lived in: uneven floor, cracked ceiling, leaky faucet, grainy TV, and furniture Goodwill probably wouldn't accept. But there was something unnaturally clean about Garth's place. It was far too organized for a normal guy. Then I noticed the girl reading in the bedroom.

"Sandy, this is Matt."

She looked up just long enough to smile a hello, then resumed her reading. Songbooks were strewn all over the coffee table: James Taylor, George Strait, Bob Seger. I sat down on an ottoman and took off my jacket.

"You sing?" he asked.

"Me? Ha ha. Not really. I sang a little in my old band, but I'm not very good."

"Think you could maybe sing some backup?"

"I can try," I said with a shrug. A guy with a beard and a guitar appeared by the screen door. "This where the audition is?" he asked, followed by a wheezy giggle and a cough.

"Come on in, Tom. Tom Skinner, this is Matt O'Meilia. He's our drummer."

Not so fast, I thought.

"Hay-lo, Matt." Tom's voice dripped with Okie drawl. Unlike most guys with such an accent, though, he didn't give me the impression he was ready to beat me into hay. He was gentle and polite, with gigantic sky-blue eyes spaced about three guitar frets apart. He was thirty-two, eight years older than Garth and me. Tom's mustache hung well over his lip, almost completely covering his mouth. After the formalities, Garth asked Tom if he'd heard the new Randy Travis song, "Diggin' Up Bones."

"Yeah, I like that tune," said Tom, taking out his guitar. "What key's it in?"

And away they went. After the first verse, I thought: this has to be the corniest song I've ever heard. But then I stopped listening to the lyrics and started listening to their voices. They sustained delicate notes. Their harmonies were impeccable. It was as though they'd been

25

singing together every day for years. They stopped when we heard the porch creaking outside. A man with a Fu Manchu mustache opened the door without bothering to knock. He was short, with light brown, unkempt hair. He sported wire-rimmed glasses, jeans, boots, and a flannel shirt, untucked. He looked like John Lennon during the Sgt. Pepper days.

"Come on in, Jed," said Garth. "This is Matt."

"I know Matt," he said. I looked at him blankly. "I used to crash your gigs at the Wavo," he explained. Then I remembered. Jed was a friend of Scott Collins and Ed Eissenstat, the other two-thirds of my recently disbanded rock trio, Tons and Tons of Hair. Nuevo Wavo, the Strip's only psychedelic venue, was one of the few places in Stillwater that allowed us to play, mostly because the club's owner happened to be our manager. Jed often showed up when we played there, his Les Paul in tow. Usually he would just barge onstage right in the middle of a song and plug into Ed's guitar amp. Tons and Tons of Hair would then suddenly get fifty watts louder and ten times better. I'd never seen Jed outside the dark and smoky interior of Nuevo Wavo, which was why I didn't recognize him. Seeing him in the light for the first time, I had trouble attaching an age to his face. He could have been twenty-five or forty-five (he was thirty-one).

"Now I remember," I said, shaking his hand and feeling comforted by the fact that someone else of rock 'n roll persuasion was present. "Screamin' Jed Lindsey."

For an hour as the three took turns suggesting songs, I listened, tapping rhythm on my knees to accompany the guitars.

"You know 'Guitars and Cadillacs?' "

"What key?"

Despite the musical material, I was fascinated by the speed and efficiency of these three. In my rock bands, a typical practice session consisted of half an hour just getting the guitars tuned, then another hour listening over and over to the song we were trying to learn. In one hour, Jed, Tom, and Garth figured out at least ten songs.

When the practice ended, I walked back home feeling uneasy. Even though it was immediately obvious that they could sing and play better than most musicians I'd associated with, it felt awkward sitting around with Garth and two old guys learning country stuff. I'd only been in bands with people of my age and ilk. But since I had to face Garth every day when I dropped by DuPree's to see Suzi, I figured it would be easier just to go along with this country thing a while, make enough money to last until graduation in May, then leave the band and Stillwater for good.

The following week, we assembled for our first full practice in a work shed in the backyard of Dale "Raddler" Shipley, one of Garth's best friends from DuPree Sports. After we had plugged in the amps and tuned up the guitars, Garth decided we'd warm up with one of his favorites.

"Let's do 'Old Time Rock 'n Roll.'"

We played without a hitch, almost. I was amused at how Garth twanged this rock 'n roll standard, but he played solid rhythm guitar and demonstrated his incredible voice control. Jed's tasteful balance of crunchy and clean riffs gave the song a full sound. Tom's bass was smooth and as dependable as a sunrise. I, however, was having problems. I was accelerating the tempo and, having been a disciple of Keith Moon, Buddy Rich, and other speed masters, was trying to throw in fancy licks where none fit, totally overdoing it, trying to show these country rubes how to play rock 'n roll.

"That was pretty good," Garth said. "But it needs to be more, you know, punchy. Crisp." In other words, I needed to play a steady beat, which was far from a requirement in my earlier bands. I'd never felt embarrassed on the drums until that cold March evening. I shook my head as I recalled telling my friends what a laugh it would be to play in a country band, how it would be so easy that I'd be able to study for tests in the middle of songs. I had doubted my desire to be in this band; suddenly I was praying I wouldn't get kicked out. To me, the only thing worse than being in a country band was not being good enough to play in one.

Throughout the practice, there was little chitchat. Garth went through the song list, showing Tom and Jed the breaks and giving me the time signature, the tempo, and some important accents. By the end of the evening, we'd learned about twenty songs. I was rapidly being introduced not only to country music but also to a serious band work ethic. For someone who had never been part of a steady group to speak of, Garth ran a mighty no-nonsense rehearsal.

Garth told us our first gig would be in a couple of weeks at Bink's, which was managed by an entrepreneurial genius named Mac Overholt. Mac had owned a tiny shotgun-style bar across the street from Willie's called Bandalero's, where he boosted beer sales by keeping a bathtub full of extra-salty peanuts for his patrons to munch all they could for free. One Wednesday night, Mac wandered over to Willie's to catch Garth's act and promptly invited him to play at Bandalero's on Tuesdays and Thursdays. Bandalero's wasn't the most performance-conducive atmosphere, with Garth having to sing above a constant din of pool balls cracking and boots crunching peanut shells, but Mac's invitation was the beginning of a long and prosperous relationship. After Bandalero's closed, Mac opened Cattle Country two blocks to the south, in the location previously occupied by the Mason Jar, a very popular bar when the Strip was in its prime. During one of Garth's gigs at Cattle Country, Mac approached Garth and told him he was going to open a big club downtown, and if Garth could put a band together, Mac would let him play there anytime he wanted to. But Bink's was quite a way off the beaten path of the Strip and the nearby campus favorite, Eskimo Joe's. It would be tough drawing the college crowd downtown where the action wasn't. Garth accepted the challenge.

"So, Garth, what's this Bink's place like?" I asked.

"Oh, it's about half country, half Greek."

I didn't know him well enough to know if he was joking or not. "You've gotta be kidding me," I said. "Rednecks and frat boys hangin' out in the same club?"

"Yep," he said, smiling. "Hell of an interestin' combination, doncha think?"

29

Tom and Jed were quite an interesting combination, too.

Tom and his younger brothers, Mike and Craig, had grown up in Bristow, Oklahoma, a prototype of Small-town, USA, about thirty minutes southwest of Tulsa. They played sports and blackened each other's eyes and rode bikes to the general store for a pop and went fishin' and huntin' and got sick from eating too many hamburgers and had lousy first dates and even lousier first kisses and went to county fairs and all the other stuff Norman Rockwell ever imagined. Ordinary. Until they stopped playing ball and started playing music.

Tom didn't touch a guitar (pronounced *GIT tar* in Bristow) until he moved to Stillwater in 1972 to enroll at OSU. He taught himself a few chords, enough to learn his first song, Neil Young's "Down By the River." He drove home one weekend to show his brothers, and soon they were infected with music fever. Mike immediately acquired a guitar and Craig bought a bass. Tom, meanwhile, was back in Stillwater prowling the Strip, listening to and learning from the abundant country and rock bands. But college life eventually overwhelmed the shy young country boy. He wasn't finding the right answers in his books or even in his guitar, so he joined the Air Force. For the next four years, he was stationed at Travis Air Force Base near San Francisco. He took his guitar along and played every spare moment the military allowed. He missed his family and his hometown, and he comforted himself by writing songs, singing them when no one was around. He discovered he could sing pretty well, and his best range was tenor. Like many servicemen, he started smoking, which added a gruff edge to his voice.

His hitch was over in 1978, and he returned to Stillwater to continue school. By then, his brothers had come a long way on their instruments. Mike had since picked up the fiddle. The three Skinners reunited in Stillwater and began performing as a trio. Tom was so impressed with Craig's ability on the bass that he bought one for himself. He started to play with other bands in Stillwater, alternating between bass and rhythm guitar.

Tom Skinner at Tulsa City Limits, 1987. Tom grew up in Bristow, Oklahoma. He thought his destiny was professional baseball until the day he saw his first serious curveball and "whiffed like a ninety-year-old woman." That's when he decided to turn his attention to music. Photo by Jana Shipley.

In 1980, the word went around the Strip that Tulsa Studios was having a talent competition, with the winner to receive free recording time. The Skinners entered and won their division. Suddenly they needed a band to do some recording. Tom recruited a lead guitarist, a drummer and, because Craig by then had moved back to Bristow, a bass player. The Skinner Brothers Band went to Tulsa and recorded nine original songs. They sent demo tapes all over the country, hoping to get recognized. Discouraged by lack of interest, the band broke up and Tom resumed his coursework, finally graduating in 1982—ten years after he'd begun—with a bachelor's degree in public relations.

In August 1983, Tom married Jeri Alexander, a girl he'd met while playing the clubs. Tom and Mike both took jobs in the mailroom at the Stillwater post office. To counter the tedium of postal life, the two got a band rolling again and landed a steady gig at Willie's on Thursday nights. For the next two years, the Skinners were a fixture on the Strip. On many of those Thursday nights, young Garth Brooks would show up and ask Tom if he could sit in for a few numbers.

Tom and Garth had met while performing in OSU's Student Union in 1982. Every Friday night, the school sponsored a pseudo-beatnik coffeehouse there called Aunt Molly's Amateur Night, where students took turns on a makeshift stage singing, telling jokes, performing skits, and reading poetry. For students too young to get into the bars or too unresourceful to acquire fake IDs, it was the perfect creative outlet. And because it was an opportunity to perform, Tom and Garth were usually there.

The Skinner Brothers were enjoying local fame, jamming with just about everyone in town because everyone in town wanted to jam with them. With each gig, their harmonies got tighter and cleaner. They started thinking about the big time, and that meant Nashville. But in the midst of planning, Jeri, with the aid of her husband, got pregnant. Nashville was thus put on hold indefinitely. In November 1985, Jeremy Skinner was born. Tom moved his young family to a smaller, more affordable apartment a block north of Eskimo Joe's.

Meanwhile, Garth had gotten over his disappointment in Nashville and was again burning with ambition and looking for a band. He knew that having one Skinner in the band would be worth any two other musicians. Not only would it make for a solid group, it would also help draw a crowd. Garth phoned Tom. Still adjusting to parenthood, Tom was reluctant to start playing again. But when Garth told him they'd be a house band and wouldn't have to travel, Tom agreed.

33

Now all the band needed was a lead guitarist. Enter Jed Lindsey.

In 1972, at age seventeen, meek and mild and unassuming David "Jed" Lindsey had departed the small, clean, quiet, friendly community of Bartlesville, Oklahoma, and plunged headfirst into its antithesis, Los Angeles, mecca for the world's greatest musicians, where the quietly self-confident guitarist hoped to join a band worthy of his talents. But the commotion, smog, glitz, and glop of LA life tore the young man's eyes wide open. Painfully homesick and frustrated by always having to lie about his age to get into the bars, he returned to Bartlesville and formed the rock group Bliss with some of his high-school pals. Jed soon became one of the best-known guitarists around. The band moved sixty miles south to Tulsa and came under the

wing of concert promoter Larry Shaeffer, owner of Cain's
Ballroom, where Bob Wills and the Texas Playboys gave
birth to western swing. Shaeffer booked Bliss at Cain's in
front of huge acts such as the Sex Pistols, REO Speed-
wagon, and Blue Oyster Cult. Although eager to become
a headline group, Bliss couldn't hold onto a lead vocalist
for more than a few months. Then Jed got a call from a
touring country singer named Mel McDaniel. He offered
Jed four hundred dollars a week plus per diem. Money and
stability had spoken: Jed shined his boots and hit the road.

After a lucrative year with McDaniel, Jed returned
to Tulsa. He hooked up with Rocking Horse, featuring
Ronnie Dunn. Jed also played with bassist/vocalist Betsy
Smittle, Garth's half-sister, in a regular gig at the Cornu-
copia Club in west Tulsa, jamming with Gus Hardin and
many other popular Tulsa performers. After a stint with
yet another band, he hit the road again, this time with
Albuquerque country singer Lanny Ross.

Constant touring and playing strained Jed's relationship with his long-time girlfriend, and they broke up in
1983. Depressed about women and tired of bands, he took
a job with a stereo-speaker manufacturer in Stillwater
called Stillwater Designs and began traveling to demonstrate Kicker speaker cabinets. Through his boss, Don
Mitchell, he met Steve and Jenny Collier, a locally popular husband-and-wife duo. They formed a band called
Steel Away, featuring Steve on steel guitar and Jenny on
the hot fiddle. One of the band's regular gigs was at Tumbleweed, a huge ballroom on the outskirts of Stillwater.
There Jed met a young bouncer named Garth Brooks.

As he did with every other band that played "the Weed,"
as it was known, Garth sat in with Steel Away. In early

34

Jed Lindsey at Tulsa City Limits, 1987. Jed grew up in Bartlesville, Oklahoma. He moved to Los Angeles immediately after graduating from high school but returned to Oklahoma when he realized the rock scene in Los Angeles was more than he could handle. He formed a band with some friends from high school and quickly established himself as one of the region's best young guitarists. Photo by Jana Shipley.

1985, Garth asked Jed if he wanted to form a band. Jed declined. Steel Away and speaker demonstrations occupied too much of his time. Jed was easily the finest guitarist around. Garth would wait.

Nearly a year later, an all-star musicians' jam took place in Perry, Oklahoma, about twenty miles west of Stillwater. It was a goodbye gig for Skinner Brothers Band drummer Ron Beckel, who was moving out of Stillwater. Among those taking turns onstage were the three Skinner brothers, Jed, and that pesky bouncer from the Weed who always seemed to materialize whenever good music was going down.

"Hey, lemme just do one more," Garth said. "How 'bout 'The Fireman.'"

Jed, Tom, Mike, and Craig looked at one another, rolled their eyes, and wondered in silent four-part harmony: When is this guy gonna quit hogging the stage?

"All right," sighed Tom. "What key?"

They launched into the George Strait standard as the crowd settled in for the long night ahead, ordering pitchers and raiding the cigarette machine. Just before his cue, the singer, bathed in cheap fluorescent light, squinted and peered beyond the stage at the smoky silhouettes helplessly nodding and tapping their fingers, arms, and feet to the rhythm of the powerful band. Then he heard his voice go tumbling toward them.

3

BINK'S

What do you get when you cross drunken fraternity brothers with drunken cowboys with a grossly under-rehearsed
band that's trying to please both groups? You get Bink's.
You also get a collection of memories—faces, events, ob-
jects, conversations—stored deep in your subconscious, to
be recalled occasionally for the rest of your life in dark,
gloomy dreams, each one more exquisitely cryptic than
the one before.

Our practice in Raddler's shed was our first and only.
The next time we got together was for our first gig, at
Bink's on a Friday night in early April. The fun began while
we were unloading the equipment from Jed's gigantic Ford
F150 SuperCab. Two fraternity guys came running out of
Bink's chasing a third. A drunken Greek tragedy unfolded
before us. The rogues caught up to their frightened prey
and one took a wild swing, hitting Jed's truck with his fist.
Garth and Tom laughed as though they were watching a

bad movie. As many fights as I'd seen, I never got used to it. My legs stiffened and my heart nearly vibrated out of my chest. The three idiots screamed and stumbled off into the night. I expected to walk into Bink's and see chairs and bottles flying, like a brawl in a John Wayne film.

I hurriedly moved my drums inside. Clean-cut, barely legal-age men and women were standing around in the pool-table area, drinking, giggling, bubbling with sexual anticipation. Some of them smoked, but it was obvious they were not experienced puffers: they held the cigarettes as far away from their bodies as possible and grimaced when taking a drag, as if getting a flu shot. An unsmiling, unshaven, darkly dressed cowboy made his way through the young college kids, silently laid two quarters on a table, and then returned to the bar area. I followed him, carrying my drums to the long, empty stage raised a foot off the dance floor. Behind it was a mirrored wall that made Bink's look twice as big as it was. Beyond the wooden rail fence that surrounded the dance floor, shadowy figures smoked and poured from pitchers of weak Oklahoma 3.2 beer, watching us move our equipment. Adjacent to the stage was the DJ booth, where a cowboy-hatted gentleman was playing the last song I expected to hear: "Heart of Rock 'n Roll" by Huey Lewis and the News.

Tom set up his bass rig stage left, Jed set up his amp stage right, and Garth placed his mike stand directly in front of my bass drum. A waitress approached.

"Y'all want somethin' to drink?" she asked.

"How much are beers?" replied Jed.

"They're free for the band," she said with a sigh, subtly warning us to not exploit this benefit.

"I'll take a Coors Light," said Jed.

I'd learned from my previous bands that drinking and drumming made me a better performer only in my mind. However, I was nervous about the band having only twenty songs to fill up four hours, and I still didn't know what to make of this place. I feared that once we began repeating songs, we'd be lynched. I asked for a beer.

"Just give me a Coke," said Garth, "and keep 'em comin'."

"I'll just take a coffee cup, ma'am," said Tom. Tom was never without his green thermos full of strong black coffee. Alcohol and Tom did not mix. During one rare binge, Tom had gone to Cain's Ballroom to see the Nitty Gritty Dirt Band. After three too many tequilas, he lost all inhibition, jumped onstage, grabbed an electric guitar, and strapped it on. Before he could strum a chord, security people swarmed like bees and literally kicked him out of the back door. And Garth, despite knowing enough drinking songs to fill fifty albums, also abstained. He avoided drinking not because of personal experience but because he was one of those rare guys who actually listened to his parents about the dangers of booze. He had seen their prophecies fulfilled many times, too, when he was rousting angry, puking cowboys at the Weed.

The waitress eyed the front of my bass drum. "What's that supposed to be?" she asked, sounding perturbed.

"That's from my old band, Tons and Tons of Hair," I said proudly, hoping she'd recognize the name. My father had created as our insignia a cosmic, three-dimensional hippie with hair cascading off into eternity.

She rolled her eyes. "That's weird." I suddenly realized we didn't have a name for our band. "Garth, what're we calling ourselves?" I asked.

39

"We're gonna be Santa Fe," he replied. We had kicked around a few names, most of them vulgar, but this was a new one.

"Why Santa Fe?" I pried. "Are you from there or something?"

"Nope, never even been there," he said, shrugging his shoulders. "It . . . just sounds good."

And that was that: an eleventh-hour band naming with no real argument from anyone. I thought it was a silly name only because it had no concrete origin—was just picked out of the blue Stillwater sky. But no one else had any better suggestions, so Santa Fe it was. At nine, after a brief sound check, we were as ready as could be. Garth, Tom, and Jed seemed calm. I was growing anxious.

40

" 'Preciate y'all bein' here tonight," Garth began. Feedback suddenly shot from the monitors straight through our brains, making us simultaneously turn our heads and grit our teeth. Feedback is one of the most detested hazards of bands, along with being shocked by ungrounded cords. Sometimes feedback can be so intense that it momentarily upsets your equilibrium and makes you nearly fall over. Tom quickly squirmed behind me, where our sound board was located, to adjust the volume and end our convulsions. Tom resumed his position, ignited a Salem, took a deep pull, set it down on his speaker cabinet, and turned to Garth for the cue to begin. Jed fired up a Merit, took a drag, and shish-kebabbed the butt on one of the strings sticking out of his pegboard.

"We're Santa Fe," Garth began, "and we're gonna start off with an ol' Randy Travis song called '1982.' Ah one—"

Garth turned around to complete the count and I stopped him.

"Wait, how's this one go?" I asked, near panic. Nerves had erased my memory.

"I'll start it off," he answered, patient despite the technical and mental difficulties. "Tom'll cue you when to come in." Garth turned to the mike.

Operator, pleeeeeez connect me . . .

Tom shot me a glance, opened his wide eyes even wider, raised his bass as if he were getting ready to shoot skeet, then brought it down as he thumped the opening three notes, which I failed to complement. Off to a great start.

To nineteeeeeeen eighty-two . . .

I eventually found my way into the song, watching Tom for cues throughout. The Bink's crowd didn't mind our ragged beginning, though, and the dance floor quickly filled. Familiar faces from DuPree Sports two-stepped by the front of the stage, smiling and winking at Garth. Garth's fiancée Sandy swept by with a rather clumsy-looking fellow about half her height. She grinned sweetly, then resumed her surveillance of the crowd, checking for cowgirls who leered just a little too suggestively at her man. She knew what a flirt he was.

The crowd wasn't exactly as Garth had described. Yes, there were Greeks and cowboys, but there were also many couples in their forties and fifties who had come to Bink's for the sole purpose of dancing all evening long. They danced because they honestly knew how to dance and wanted to dance, not just arbitrarily throw themselves around simply because the beer and the rhythm

41

commanded them to do so, as in the rock clubs I'd played, where people never danced before ten o'clock, never before the band had played at least one set, and never before they had a good buzz.

Jed was staring straight ahead, his slight grin fixed as though he were reading the morning funnies, rarely even glancing at his guitar, his mind sending precise chord-pattern instructions to his nimble fingers. Tom monitored the neck of his bass carefully, frequently licking the bottom of his mustache, his facial expressions as erratic as Jed's were unchanging. Garth tapped his boot along as he sang, bending his knees to embellish high notes. With every lyric, a wisp of second-hand smoke was ejected from his mouth. He used an elastic guitar strap for his round-backed Ovation, enabling him to stretch the guitar down below his waist if he felt like it, which he did often, probably to vent nervous energy.

Tom and Garth harmonized the final chorus, their voices blending perfectly. Garth turned around, gave everyone a slight nod, then raised and dropped the neck of his guitar. Santa Fe song number one was a wrap. Without applause, the crowd returned to their tables, to the bar, to the pool room. I was a little miffed, expecting at least a conciliatory clap from a few people. I later came to understand that most of the crowds we played for came not to see a show but to *be* a show. They gathered to participate in the odd ritual of moving in circles within circles within circles, with heavy carcasses of cattle, snake, ostrich, kangaroo, buffalo, alligator, lizard, elephant, anteater, caribou, anaconda, and deer attached to their feet. The band's mission was to complement their choreography. We were simply a recreational tool—a living, breathing, smoking, drinking jukebox.

Tom sipped coffee, Jed and I swigged brew, and Garth pulled a nasal spray out of his pocket and took a snort. "Damn allergies," he said, checking the song list. "Lessee, how 'bout 'Guitars and Cadillacs?'"

"How's this one go?" I asked again, as I would for each song the rest of the evening. For me, our first show at Bink's was like pulling teeth. But as the evening wore on, we began to get a sense of each other's styles, as well as each other's habits: sip, swig, smoke, snort. I worried about Garth. He was really putting away the Neo-Synephrine. I imagined his nasal passages to look like abandoned strip mines.

At exactly 9:45, we finished the first set. "Fifteen minutes, boys," Garth announced. "Back here at ten." The DJ jumped into his booth and put on "Nasty Girl," a song routinely played between sets for the dancers who just couldn't get enough. Everyone, including the waitresses, assembled on the dance floor and began a country-style line dance, which looked like the old Bus Stop from the disco days.

Western decor, rock music, frat boys fighting, country folk disco dancing—Bink's made no sense to me. "This place is bizarre, Garth," I said as we walked over toward the bar.

"Glad you like it, man," he laughed. "Here's the brains behind it all."

Mac Overholt approached us. "I thought you boys sounded reeeel good," he said.

"Thanks, Mac," Garth replied, proceeding to introduce us. A ruggedly handsome man, Mac was then about forty-five, with dark, graying hair which he slicked over with

43

Mac Overholt, 1995. An extraordinary promoter, Mac owned several bars in Stillwater, the last one being Bink's. Among his ideas for attracting patrons were wet T-shirt contests and lingerie shows. To sell more beer at his bars, he used to provide extra-salty peanuts for his patrons. Photo by Millie Overholt.

greasy kid stuff. His accent was pure small-town Oklahoma. He wore a short-sleeved knit shirt, circa 1976, with those infamously obvious collars that must have been designed by some nearsighted aircraft engineer. Peeking through the polyester was a sizeable potbelly, the result of a silo's worth of bar chips and burgers he fried up regularly

44

in the Bink's kitchen. Perhaps it was the slow migration of flesh to his midsection that robbed Mac of buttocks. Whatever the cause, his jeans hung precariously, threatening at any moment to slip to the floor. He motioned over an old man who resembled Pistol Pete, the OSU Cowboy mascot.

"Boys, I'd like you to meet Bink."

Jed and I looked at each other and thought the same thing: There's someone really named Bink?

"Howdy," Bink said, predictably. Edmund D. "Bink" Simank Sr. was co-owner of the club with Mac and two other men. At sixty-four, he had a short, stooped frame and a huge gray mustache. But it was his voice we noticed first: not merely whiskey-and-cigarette-stained, it was the voice of gravel being mixed in a cement truck. Upon hearing him speak, I expected Tom and Jed to quit smoking on the spot. In time, the other thing we would notice about Bink was that he was usually arm in arm with some lovely and much younger woman.

"Showtime," said Garth. Jed and I dashed to the bar for refreshments, then joined Tom and Garth onstage. Garth wore Tom's bass. "Tom's gonna start us out," he said.

Tom put on his electric guitar and stepped up to the mike. "We're gonna do a coupla Rodney Crowell tunes for ya," he announced. Crowell was one of Tom's many non-mainstream songwriting heroes, along with John Prine, Guy Clark, Doc Watson, and Ricky Skaggs. "I'll kick it off," he told me, "and you watch Garth to come in."

Garth, looking rather unnatural with a bass in his arms, yielded the spotlight to Tom and stood squarely in front of my kit, facing me, his legs wide apart as if he were balancing barbells. He was poised like a soldier, concentrating

mightily on the frets and, as if it were bass-playing protocol, his tongue was magnetized to the bottom of his
mustache. We kicked off "Ain't Livin' Long Like This,"
beginning at the same time, for once. Because he stood
next to me throughout the song, I was given my first
opportunity to study the Garth face in performance.
Concentration has a unique effect on any musician's expression. If you've ever watched a four-year-old play with
Legos, you can begin to understand the intensity. With
each note, Garth's face reflected bliss, wonder, triumph,
surprise, mischief: *I just won the lottery, I just scored the winning touchdown, I just learned how babies are made, I just fell in
love.* His face and his entire body were in perpetual motion.
He walked, he jogged, he strutted with mock heavy-metal
bravado, his wrists bending mechanically, his fingers moving fitfully but efficiently—singing or playing, he never
missed a note that I can remember—succeeding in making
the difficult transition from the relatively delicate strings
of his Ovation to the thick cables of the bass.

I couldn't help but wonder if I were witnessing musical zeal personified or feigned exuberance designed to
excite the crowd and the band. Because I did not understand the appeal of country music, I was at first skeptical
of Garth's performance within a performance. I thought
it was hokey, that Garth was a poseur. To my right, the
stoic, road-tough Jed, yet another Merit burning between
his lips, was calmly tearing through a solo, emanating pro-
totypical rock cool, daring anyone to enter his sphere, his
blazing licks guarding him like Dobermans. Tom turned
around to watch, smiling and shaking his head admiringly,
watching Jed's fingers sizzle, as he was fond of saying, "like
spiders on a hot skillet." Garth, two hundred pounds of

46

gooseflesh, waltzed over to share Jed's moment, the Garth face broadcasting awe, then disbelief, then *you son-of-a-gun, you*, his every emotion naked, begging the band, the dancers, Bink, Mac, anyone and everyone to dash madly into his personal musical kingdom.

This was country music? This was what I was so reluctant to be part of, the stuff I felt I was betraying rock 'n roll for? By the end of the evening, my doubts about Garth's sincerity and intensity had vanished. I came to realize that I was the only poseur onstage, the tempo-erratic basher of nylon and brass, pretending to be in the same league as my cohorts who communicated to one another in the beautiful, mysterious languages of scale, chord progression, and harmony. I was fluent only in the language of garage-bandism, and that evening I demonstrated my mastery of it. With sticks inadvertently flying out of my sweaty palms and my drum kit sliding all over the slick wooden stage, on this platform of professionals I was the essence of amateurism.

47

By the middle of the third set, we'd run out of songs. But because Garth, Jed, and Tom knew the language of music, we were able to finish out the evening without having to stall noticeably.

"You know 'Fire and Rain'?" Garth asked Tom.

"What key?" came the familiar reply.

Some of the dancers approached the stage and whispered to Garth.

"Hey, Tom, you know 'Tennessee Waltz'?"

"I think so. What key?"

Someone asked for the Eagles' "Peaceful Easy Feeling." Tom had played this song with the Skinner Brothers Band so many times that he could barely stand even hearing it again. But trooper that he was, and because we were hurting for material, he sucked it up and led the way. Throughout the history of Santa Fe, never was a song requested by the audience that either Garth or Tom didn't know or hadn't at least heard. Every night we played a song that we'd never done together, and invariably we'd nail it from beginning to end. Audiences began to take it for granted that we simply knew every song ever written. "How 'bout a slow one?" ol' Billy Joe or Jim Bob would ask. "You got it," Garth would say with a wink, then proceed to pull some obscure tune from the 1940s out of his hat, some ballad Gene Autry had done while sitting around a campfire in a B movie. Garth had an amazing talent for remembering lyrics. Tom was just as good at dredging up some old bluegrass or gospel number. Garth would usually know the song, too, and join in on the chorus, always the right harmony, always in perfect pitch, with Jed tastefully filling the gaps while my eyes ping-ponged among my bandmates, waiting for cues like an actor with a poor memory, trying desperately not to ruin the mood. Over the next few months, though, I became a steadier drummer than I ever thought possible. Playing in Santa Fe, it was as inevitable as learning table manners after marrying royalty.

48

Our Bink's deal required the band to play Friday, Saturday, and Monday nights as a quartet, and on Tuesdays as the Jed-Tom-Matt trio, serving as the backing group for Bink's Tuesday night local talent showcase. Garth played solo on Tuesdays, either at Willie's or at some other joint on the Strip. Not a great deal of local talent showed up on Tuesdays, and those who did were usually either embarrassingly overconfident or just downright awful, or both. Sometimes Jed's old Steel Away bandmates Steve and

Edmund D. "Bink" Simank, 1995. Bink was unable to locate any photos of himself back when Bink's was in existence or of the club itself, which is now a second-hand furniture store. When his mustache was in full bloom, he was a dead ringer for Pistol Pete, the OSU Cowboys mascot. Photo by the author.

Jenny Collier sat in with us. Playing with seven or eight different performers a night helped us develop our musical instincts. We learned to read not only one another's lips but also the subtle cues of eyes, eyebrows, mouths, elbows, and feet. Within each song was a Santa Fe symphony of anatomy.

When Talent Night failed to get any better, Mac and Bink concocted two other ways to draw a crowd on Tuesdays: lingerie shows and wet T-shirt contests. Not surprisingly, we started seeing our biggest and certainly most buxom crowds on Tuesday nights. The Santa Fe trio would play a set or two, then out came the ladies, and out came the beasts from within our relatively tame audience. The lingerie shows were positively shameless: gorgeous women "marketing" bedroom wear, seductively parading around the dance floor while grown men succumbed to their primal instincts and yelped like dogs. Though one couldn't tell it by the quivering grin on my face, I felt sorry for the girls, for the leering cowboys, for Mac and Bink, for humanity.

Meanwhile, down on the Strip, Garth was probably wondering where his loyal fans were disappearing to on Tuesday nights. He got a chance to see for himself when one of his solo gigs got canceled and he showed up to play. After two sets, Mac took the stage and announced a wet T-shirt contest. A Bink's waitress with the ironically wholesome name of Susie made the dreams of every male in the audience come true by agreeing to participate. Susie was a knockout blonde, beautiful of face and quite architecturally sound. To go along with her handsome physique was a powerfully complex personality. She had a mind like Mae West and a mouth like a sailor. She teased her admirers, pinching their behinds and casually brushing up against them with various soft parts of her torso. She intimidated most of the guys at Bink's, although we pretended otherwise. Her every movement, every utterance inspired filthy, dirty, grimy thoughts. And when the word went around the bar that Susie was going to "compete" for the prize of Best Wet Chest, even the most reserved of patrons found themselves migrating toward the showroom floor to find the best view possible.

Mac appointed reluctant Tom and agreeable Jed as judges. Garth and I sat on the stage and giggled along with the rest of the perverts who surrounded the dance floor and created a sexual boxing ring. Three other girls, encouraged by beer and boyfriends, challenged Susie. The participants lined up. First a murmur, than a loud cho-

50

rus of "Skin to win!" arose. The DJ cued "Nasty Girl," and the real nasty girls lubricated their shirts. For the next ten minutes, Bink's became Bourbon Street during Mardi Gras. The contestants writhed, acting their sexiest. First, boots were shed, followed by socks. Belts were removed and jeans jettisoned. Two had had enough, collected their clothes, and vanished meekly into the crowd. "Skin to win!" shouted the Greeks and cowboys, most laughing but some bordering on anger. The girl who dared to match bods with Susie was slight of frame and rather flat, but wasn't the least self-conscious about it. Susie, growing more and more annoyed by the oglers and her overachieving competitor, finally whisked off her top to a thunderous roar. But it wasn't over yet, as her rival answered by discarding her shirt *and* panties, sending the mesmerized audience into seizures. Sensing her victory slipping away, Susie yielded to the pressure and flung her undies into the crowd and raised her arms in triumph, claiming her seemingly rightful crown. Off in the shadows, Mac beamed proudly: he had brought the Strip to Bink's.

51

Two completely naked women and a hundred pairs of bulging eyeballs turned to the stage for the judges' decision. Tom and Jed whispered nervously to each other, nodded, and then whispered to Mac, who then approached the mike: "The judges have decided that the fifty-dollar prize be split." Fair enough. After all, how were Tom and Jed, mere musicians, able to judge the quality of one's nakedness over another's without embarrassing someone? But Susie was not so understanding. She went into a tirade, screaming at the top of her considerable lungs, cursing the judges, Mac, Bink, and the panting, flabbergasted crowd, clumsily gathering up her wardrobe in the process, wondering what deviant had made off with her underwear, sobbing and damning everyone to hell: "Twenty-five bucks to see this body? Fifty bucks, maybe, but twenty-five? Fuck every fucking one of you fuckers!"

Susie fled the bar in tears. Garth decided we'd better strike up the band immediately to try to return the place to normal. But first we had to round up Jed and Tom, who had escaped to the parking lot to wait for the storm to blow over. We started playing, the dancers took the place of the striptease, and Bink's was calm again. By the end of the evening, though, everyone in the bar still had a rather unpeaceful, uneasy feeling.

The band gathered at Bink's early the following Friday night to practice a song that Garth and his rodeo buddy Randy Taylor had written, called "Much Too Young to Feel This Damn Old." While we were setting up the equipment, Mac told us that Susie, that bubbling, fragile mixture of humor, beauty, sensual mischief, and anger, had committed suicide the night before. The Bink's employees were all sniffles and somber stares. We hadn't known Susie very well or for very long. She had obviously had some pretty awful problems. But we'd all been part of that disturbing Tuesday evening and felt vaguely responsible.

The show went on. We inaugurated "Much Too Young," playing it stiffly but passably, not sure of the arrangement. A few people clapped politely. Garth sensed that it needed something, perhaps another instrument, another voice.

Tom's brother Mike would fill the void a few weeks later. After graduating from high school, Mike Skinner had elected not to follow his brother to OSU or the Air Force. Instead, he joined a workers' union in Bristow and began a short career as a pipefitter. Wanderlust took him to Lake Charles, Louisiana. With his fiddle he wiled away the hours after the day's backbreaking toil, sitting in his tiny apartment with the window open, a small fan providing scant relief from the Louisiana heat and humidity. Far away from his home and his family, Mike listened to the radio and, with the same calloused, oily fingers that manhandled machines all day long, caressed his delicate instrument, coaxing from it unearthly sweet, melancholy tones that defined his loneliness.

Despite his musical gifts, his easy humor, his handsome features—long, golden locks, barrel chest, baby-blue eyes and thick blonde mustache—Mike was the least self-confident of the Skinners. While growing up, Mike, like me, had had bad luck with bullies. In the middle of a high-school science class, one of Mike's classmates, tripping violently on LSD, had blindsided him with a punch to the upper jaw, sending four of his teeth shooting across the floor. Such events tend to make one skittish about life, particularly if one is sensitive in nature. That and other occurrences—constant warring with Tom and Craig, for example—caused him to be in perpetual doubt about his talents, his destiny.

53

But he was intuitive enough to realize that he didn't belong in Cajun country, and after a year and a half he moved back to Bristow and eventually joined Tom in Stillwater, renting a duplex no larger than the average bathroom, about twenty yards from Garth's back door and about forty yards from my house. He was characteristically hesitant when Garth knocked on his door one day in early May and asked him to join the group.

"Well, shoot, I don't know, Garth," Mike said.

"C'mon, man," Garth said, "I—*we* need you. We need harmonies and, well, we just need a fuller sound."

Mike stared at the ground, shaking his head, then finally looked up. "Where y'all playin' next?" he sighed. "I'll come check it out."

Another band was playing at Bink's the following weekend, so Garth booked us at a club south of town called the Sundowner, the darkest, dankest sanctuary of chain-smoking, weather-beaten, leather-skinned, whiskey-quaffing cowboys Edgar Allan Poe could ever have imagined. The faint light from the table candles—those red, oblong globes with the fabric webbing—struggled in vain to cut through the murk. A few neon beer signs guided the way to the watering hole at the rear of the bar, opposite the stage, where a craggy, bearded curmudgeon with hands and fingers the color and texture of cooked sausage dispensed drinks with a grunt and a wheeze. On the walls in the pool room was a half-finished mural of the old West: buffaloes, tumbleweeds, proud Indian warriors, cowboys on horseback, and a glorious sunset they prepared to ride off into. Tom had played the Sundowner before and dubbed it Honky-Tonk Hell. "We played a month here one weekend," he said. That was where Mike saw us play for the first time, and that was when he decided, in a fleeting moment of self-confidence, that maybe the band could use his help. "Shoot," he deadpanned, "to play fine establishments such as this, I'd be a fool not to hook up with you fellas."

With the addition of Mike, our song list expanded. Any song featuring the fiddle—such as "Milk Cow Blues,"

"Cotton-eyed Joe," and anything from the Charlie Daniels anthology—was ours to cover. Plus, if we felt like countrifying anything from our rock repertoire, Garth gave Mike the nod, often unexpectedly, even on such rockers as "Old Time Rock 'n Roll," "Take the Money and Run," and "Wipeout," songs with tempos that aren't exactly fiddle-friendly. Like an ill-prepared schoolboy called to the chalkboard, Mike would scramble through the solo, shaking his head in disgust throughout. When Mike would confess his awkwardness about invading guitar territory with fiddle, Garth would nod understandingly, pat Mike on the back, and reassure him that he'd never put the humblest of Skinners in an embarrassing performance situation again. But Garth's interpretation of "embarrassing" was broad, to say the least. To Garth, "embarrassing" was returning from Nashville twenty-three hours after having told everyone you were going to be the greatest singer since Hank Sr. Playing a fiddle solo during a rock song was merely challenging.

From every viewpoint but his own, Mike and his fiddle—along with harmonizing precision that would make a Mormon choirboy envious—gave the band the much-needed dimension Garth desired. In an eerie episode one Friday before a Bink's gig, Mike proved that his membership in Santa Fe would be invaluable. We had assembled early at the bar to practice "Much Too Young." Garth suggested Mike play a fiddle intro. Garth strummed the opening. Mike put fiddle to chin and cocked his bow, listening intently, closing his eyes. He struck the strings and a hollow, almost mournful strain filled the empty bar. Garth stopped playing and waved the rest of us off.

"What's wrong?" Mike asked nervously.

"Man, Mike," Garth gushed, "that is fucking *it!*"

Emphasizing the statement was a Garth face we hadn't seen: crazed grin, quivering cheekbones, eyes as big and glassy as a stuffed owl's—like a man possessed, by God or the devil or maybe even Hank Williams himself. None of us, not even Garth, could tell which one it was.

4

Show Biz

Perhaps there is a band of pygmies in deepest, darkest Africa that has yet to hear the tale of how Garth Brooks met his wife. In this age of excessive information, surely everyone has heard the story so many times that they can recite it as automatically as their telephone number. As the legend goes, when Garth was a bouncer at the Weed, someone told him two girls were duking it out in the powder room. Garth rushed in to find a tall, blonde, exceedingly irate tomboy with her fist wedged in Sheetrock, the result of a drunken roundhouse aimed at her target's jawbone. Garth helped free her hand, bells and whistles went off in their heads, and a duo now nearly as famous as John and Yoko began their courtship.

The weekend following Mike's debut, Santa Fe did not play because Garth and Sandy were tying the knot in Owasso, Oklahoma, Sandy's hometown. It was a small ceremony, with mostly family members in attendance. The next weekend, it was business as usual at Bink's. Garth returned sporting a week's worth of beard. His face was not only in constant transition onstage, it was also always in various stages of growth. He changed the hair on his face as often as some neurotic people rearrange their furniture. One week he'd have mustache, two weeks later a mustache and beard, a month later just the mustache again, then he'd shave off the whole mess and start over.

The newlyweds moved two doors south, into my old house, and I moved back to my parents' house in Tulsa, my first summer at home in several years. I had originally planned to dump the band after graduation, but Garth had gigs lined up all summer that would pay a lot better and be less work than mowing lawns or cleaning dog kennel cages or any of the other brainless summer jobs I usually scrounged up. So I decided to spend that summer hiding from my father during the week and then sneaking off to Stillwater on Fridays for weekends in the country. Sometimes I slept on the floor of Mike's cramped apartment, and other times on a couch in my old living room, the guest of my gracious but rather eccentric hosts, Mr. and Mrs. Garth Brooks.

In a town of mostly drab, white A-frames, the house in which Garth and Sandy first lived as a married couple was unusual because of its bright lemon-yellow exterior. Colored paint was a luxury for which most Stillwater landlords would never spare expense, as were such extravagant items as adequate heating, air conditioning, effective plumbing, and nonstained, nongold shag carpet. Downstairs there were two wall heaters, only one of which worked, to heat approximately a thousand square feet. The downstairs bedroom, where I lived during the first semester, required

a mobile heating unit, which to poor college students usually meant the cheapest space heater money could buy, the
kind that sapped electricity from the whole block when
turned on and that is probably responsible for more house-
hold fires than any other causes except arson and falling
asleep while smoking. Many a cold night I went to sleep,
only to rise at three in the morning frozen solid because
my little heater had caused a fuse meltdown. But upstairs,
where I was fortunate to be able to move in my second
semester, heat was overabundant. In Garth and Sandy's
bedroom, formerly mine, a monstrous heater had to be
cranked in order to heat the bedroom across the hall and
the bathroom. During winter, one thus had the choice
of freezing downstairs or sweating upstairs—no middle
ground. It was the perfect metaphorical home for Garth.
The sad thing is, as big a lemon as the lemon-yellow house   59
on South Duck Street was, it was by a mile the nicest of
the six Stillwater residences I inhabited.

    After a Bink's gig one Friday night, Garth and I returned
to his house at about 2:00 A.M. He and Sandy went up
to bed and I lay on the couch, my ears ringing from four
hours of cymbal smashing and Jed's high-decibel leads. No
matter how tired I was, it was never easy going straight to
sleep after a show. The noise and commotion ricocheted
around in my head for at least an hour afterward. Trying
to get comfortable on Garth's quicksand couch, I lay on
my right, then left. *Breeeeeep.* A cricket had found its way
into the living room. I cursed it and rolled over. No more
cricket sound. I rolled again. *Breeeeeep.* As I rolled left then
right over and over, I began to notice that I could hear the
confounded insect only when my left ear was exposed. I
was well aware of and quite paranoid about the effects of

long-term exposure to loud music, having played in ob-
noxiously loud bands for five years. Once I volunteered
to help test new auditory equipment at OSU's speech and
hearing clinic and learned that my right ear had sustained
a 60 percent loss in high-frequency hearing. As I lay there
in the dark, cupping my hand over my right ear then my
left, wondering how difficult it would be to learn sign language, a light upstairs clicked on and Garth and Sandy
came loping down.

"What're you guys doing?" I asked.

"We can't sleep," Garth said.

"Is it the cricket?" I asked.

They squinted, shook their heads, and shuffled into the
kitchen. I heard the clanking of dishes, a box being ripped
open, ice bouncing into glasses, and the deflation of a pop
bottle. Like zombies, Garth and Sandy moved into the
dining room and placed on the table two bowls, each large
enough to toss a salad in, a box of Cap'n Crunch, and two
large glasses of Coke. I got up.

"What in the hell are you all doing?"

"When we can't sleep," Garth said in between chomps,
"we eat."

"You mean you can eat and drink nothing but pure sugar
and caffeine and then go to sleep?" I asked, dumbfounded.

"Works every time," said Sandy. "Want some?"

"No thanks. I'll wait 'til morning."

I sank back into the couch and listened to the Brookses
chomp and slurp and snort. They spoke not a word, they
just ate. The potion finally began to work. They got up
from the table, stretched, yawned, mumbled good night,
and lumbered up the stairs. In a few minutes, I heard alternating snores as loud as chain saws. The cricket had left,
probably to feast on the sugary remains in the other room.

60

I rolled onto my left side and placed my good ear down on the pillow, blocking out the clamor upstairs. Being deaf, it occurred to me that morning, has its advantages.

Garth announced the next week at Bink's that we were going to appear on an Oklahoma City television program called *A.M. Oklahoma.*

"All right!" went up the Santa Fe cheer.

"There's only one catch," continued Garth. "We'll be playing live—at six-thirty in the morning."

"Ugh!" went up the Santa Fe groan.

How Garth finagled many of our gigs was a complete mystery to me. I stopped asking how or why, only when and where. At that point, I had decided some things were better left unexplained. Garth named the band, Garth got the gigs. Why *were* we called Santa Fe? Who cared? I was making more than two hundred bucks a week, which I considered a mountain of money at the time, for merely slapping the drums around. That was good enough for me.

We loaded Jed's truck the night before our TV debut. We rose at 3:00 A.M. and assembled at Garth's house. He had breakfast ready for anyone who needed a sugar rush. I took him up on the Cap'n Crunch but passed on the Coke, opting instead for some of Tom's 30-weight Folger's. I piled into the truck with Jed and Tom, Mike hopped into Garth's GMC Jimmy, and we left at four. We arrived at the station at five-thirty, and started setting up on the KTVY stage.

A.M. Oklahoma was hosted by brothers Ben and Butch McCain. It was your basic morning show, with tips on

how to winterize your car, start a bonsai garden, and protect yourself from credit-card fraud. Butch greeted us with
an enthusiasm not characteristic of normal human be-
ings at that hour. Sleepiness and the excitement of being
on TV canceled each other out and put us all in a fairly
calm state of mind. Back in Stillwater, the folks at DuPree
Sports, Jeri Skinner, and Sandy Brooks were gathering
sleepily around their TV sets. In nearby Yukon, Colleen
and Troyal Brooks were nervously frying up the bacon and
putting on the coffee, giddy from the anticipation of seeing their son play to his biggest audience ever. Only they
and Sandy really knew how much it meant to Garth to be
playing on TV in his hometown.

Garth decided we'd open with Charlie Daniels's "Drinking My Baby Goodbye" and end with George Strait's
"Nobody in His Right Mind," an appropriate tune for
any band playing at 6:30 A.M. After a quick meeting with
Butch—brother Ben was gone that day—we were told to
take our places.

"Here we go, Butch," announced the director. "In five,
four, three . . ."

Butch straightened his jacket and donned his TV smile.
"Say, here's a group I know you're gonna enjoy. From
Stillwater, America, they're called Santa Fe!"

The second Butch finished talking, we crashed in together. Jed tore through the opening riff, which segued
into Mike's sixteen-bar fiddle lead, allowing Garth plenty
of time to clear the Coke phlegm out of his throat and tell
all the folks out there in TV land:

> Well, I'm sittin' on a bar stool
> Actin' like a durn fool
> That's what I'm a doin' today.

We hadn't had much time to do a sound check, so we had to rely on the KTVY engineers to give us a good mix. The stage equipment was pretty crude, about as prehistoric as ours, so we had no idea how it was going to sound to the people watching. As it turned out, the mix was excellent. Garth shifted his voice and face into performance gear, Tom harmonized with precision, I didn't drop any sticks, Mike stepped in and ripped a couple of great leads that he of course thought were horrible, and Jed, even without the lubrication of a few Coors Lights, ignited a small fire on the neck of his Gibson. It actually looked as if we knew what we were doing. At the end of the song, the camera whipped over to Butch, who was applauding along with the technical crew and various other *A.M Oklahoma* personnel who had peeked into the studio to see what all the racket was.

"Yeah!" said Butch. "All right! That music makes me wanna *dance*! Good job, fellas." And with that our TV debut was over. We went offstage for more coffee and orange juice while we watched Butch do a scintillating report on America's top models. A stagehand appeared and told us to get ready for our second song. Butch approached.

"When we go back on," he told Garth, "I'm gonna ask you to introduce everyone." "Sure thing, Butch," said Garth, who then turned to Jed and handed over his big white Stetson. "Here, you wear this." Garth stuck a DuPree Sports ball cap on his own head. The little red light on top of the camera came on, and we all gulped in unison. Butch switched to his interviewer mode.

"I'm here with Santa Fe on *A.M. Oklahoma*, talking with Garth Brooks. Say, you fellas sure can pick and play. How long you been together?"

"About four days now," Garth said, which made

everyone yuk-yuk and loosen up a little.

"No, come on, tell the truth."

"Well, us four have been together about two months, and we just picked up Mike, over there on the fiddle."

Garth introduced Jed, then me. "And over here on bass is Tom Skinner, and his brother, Mike Skinner."

"And Lynyrd, your cousin," chimed in our lightning-quick-witted host. Even though it was only a low-grade pun—Mike and Tom had heard Lynyrd Skynyrd wise-cracks about their surname a thousand times—all of us guffawed as if it was the funniest cotton-pickin' thang we'd ever heard. I'd always wondered why TV studio audiences laugh their heads off at even the lamest of jokes. I found out that morning. When you're around show biz folks, you turn into show biz folks.

Butch asked us what we did for a living. Garth slowly bowed his head and displayed the DuPree Sports logo on his cap. "I work for, uh . . . ," he said slowly, pointing to his cap as the camera zoomed in on it, "DuPree Sports."

"Oh, I see, you've got a sporting goods store there in Stillwater," said Butch, who seemed a little taken off guard. Such blatant plugs probably were not allowed by the KTVY management, but since we were live it was too late to do anything about it. Back in Stillwater, DuPree Sports owners Ed and Ann Watkins were grinning ear to ear over their free advertising. Whether they put Garth up to it or it brought them any new business, I don't know.

Butch posed the occupational question to Jed, who replied, "I'm just a musician."

"*Just* a musician, huh?" Butch echoed with a knowing nod to the camera. Butch and his brother Ben had a lit-tle singing act of their own, a kind of slicked-up Haggar

Twins thing. "And what about you?" he asked me. I didn't have any life to speak of. I didn't want to say I was a musician because I was only a drummer. Nor did I want to say I was a philosophy graduate because no one would have cared.

"I run a vegetable stand out on the highway," I said, thinking I was going to fluster our double-breasted master of ceremonies.

"Oh, yeah," replied Butch without skipping a beat, "I think I bought a watermelon from you once. And you?"

"I'm a postman," said Tom, smirking at all the lies flying around.

The mike went to Mike. "I'm also a postman," he said. Butch couldn't think of anything clever to say about two brothers with the same occupation, so he just induced a TV laugh, then turned to Garth and asked if we were going to do another song, as if it weren't planned.

"We're gonna do that new one by George Strait, called 'Nobody in His Right Mind.' "

"OK," said Butch, relieved the interview was over. "Once again, here's Santa Fe."

Jed kicked us off and we glided into the melancholy number, which ran just a little bit over time and got cut off by the credits. All in all, it was a very good gig. Garth got to show thousands of people in Oklahoma City and Stillwater the quality of his voice, and Butch was so impressed with the band that he scheduled us to play on the show later that summer.

The second time we played on *A.M. Oklahoma* wasn't as pleasant. Butch's brother Ben was back on the set, and before the show he pulled Garth aside and asked him if we would play a September variety show in which he and

Garth, summer, 1986, when he was making a name for himself as the leader of the best band in Stillwater. Photo credit: *Stillwater NewsPress.*

Butch were somehow involved. Garth said he'd have to check our schedule. When Ben tried to put the squeeze on him to commit, Garth politely said that we'd have to think about it.

We took the stage and did Dwight Yoakam's "Guitars and Cadillacs." We sounded good enough in the studio, but the broadcast mix was so bad that all the television audience could hear were Garth's voice, my bass drum, and Mike's fiddle. It was embarrassing. To make matters worse, after we finished playing Ben announced, "Those fellas will be with us at the Oklahoma Variety Show on September sixth at Stage Center. We look forward to that." In unison we turned to Garth with dumb looks on our faces.

"What's all that about the Oklahoma Variety Show?" Tom asked Garth after we went backstage.

"It's not true," Garth assured us. "Ben's trying to pressure us into a show I told him we can't commit to yet. I guess he figured we'd cave in and do it if he announced it like that, but he's dead wrong."

Ben suddenly appeared. "Say, fellas, how 'bout doing that 'Nobody in His Right Mind' tune you did last time? Butch said you guys did it really well and I'd like to hear it."

"Well, Ben, that's nice of Butch to say, but we were hoping it'd be all right if we did this original song of ours," replied our diplomatic singer, finding the strength to suppress his desire to punch Ben's lights out.

"Garth, everyone here would really like you to do 'Nobody in His Right Mind,'" the unbending Ben said flatly, then left without giving Garth time for rebuttal. We seriously considered ignoring Ben and doing "Much Too Young" as we'd planned. At that point, we didn't care if

67

KTVY asked us back again or not. But at the last second, Garth decided we should bite our collective tongue and go ahead and play the George Strait tune. A band so young and full of ambition couldn't afford to start burning bridges. Our diplomacy was all for naught, however; KTVY never called us again.

———————————————

Other than one encounter with the ugly side of TV, it was a great summer. Through Tulsa's Little Wing Productions and Jim Halsey Management, Mac corralled some of the biggest names in country music, past and present, to perform at tiny Bink's, and we opened for all of them. Our first big opening was on a Thursday night in June for Dwight Yoakam, who was touring to promote his "Guitars and Cadillacs" album. Santa Fe covered about half the songs from that album, so we were excited about fronting this mysterious, tight-jeaned singer who was considered one of the symbols of the newer, hipper country music scene.

When I drove into the Bink's parking lot, the Yoakam touring bus was backed up to the door. I parked and made my way into the club. Garth was standing outside the door talking to a middle-aged man and a real skinny guy wearing a cowboy hat pulled practically down to his nose. I gave Garth a nod and walked in past the equipment, which filled half the club. I wondered how we were going to get our stuff and Yoakam's all on the same stage. Jed approached.

"Has Mac talked to you yet?" he asked.

"No, I just got here."

"Well, Mac wanted all of us to know that we can't take any pictures of Dwight."

68

"What?"

"That's what he said."

"What's the big deal?" I asked. "Is he an Indian or something?"

"What do you mean?"

"Some Indians don't like their pictures taken because they think it steals their soul."

"I don't think so," he said, thinking I was being serious. "He doesn't *look* Indian."

"Then maybe he's a vampire and he doesn't want anyone taking his picture because it won't show up."

"I don't know," said Jed, not offering to help me speculate as to why on earth someone would insist that no one take his picture. "Just don't do it."

"What'll happen if I do? Will I be killed?"

Jed finally smiled. "Probably."

It turned out that the skinny guy talking to Garth outside was Dwight. His picture phobia may have had something to do with not wanting evidence that he played in a little bar in Stillwater after having been on the *Tonight* show just a few evenings earlier. Mac had booked Dwight in April, when his "Guitars and Cadillacs" album hadn't yet taken off. By June, though, "Honky Tonk Man" was a huge single and Dwight had become one of the most popular performers in the country. But a contract's a contract. I thought about going outside to introduce myself to him, meet a big star and everything, but decided not to. What would I have said? I wasn't exactly a fan. In fact, I'd never heard any of his songs before I played them with Santa Fe. I concluded that I probably couldn't have a normal conversation with someone so afraid to have his picture taken. So I just got a beer and sat down with Tom, Jed, and Mike, and watched the Yoakam crew maneuver the equipment and run miles of cables all over the place.

"Where am I gonna put my drums?" I asked Tom.

"I think you're gonna use their drummer's kit."

"I wish someone would have told me that before I hauled mine over here." It was a sourpuss thing to say, but I was disappointed I couldn't use my drums. Every drummer is particular about his precious skins. Every kit is different, and none ever sounds as good as your own. When you have to use another guy's set, he invariably demands that you don't move anything out of place. If you do, he gets angry and acts as if you have completely screwed up his life. But it's hard not to do a little adjusting. Some guys have arms like orangutans and put their cymbals seven feet high. Then there are the power drummers, who place the toms a foot apart and keep the heads so loose that you practically need a baseball bat to make any noise. Other guys like to bury themselves behind a big row of toms and have twelve cymbals pointed in every possible direction. I always set my kit up jazz-style, very compact, with super-tight heads that gave a loud, crisp report at the slightest touch. Dwight Yoakam's drummer had one of the most awkward setups I'd ever seen. So when the time came to do a sound check, I got behind the skins, pulled out my drum key, and started arranging everything to my liking.

"Hey, man, I wouldn't do that if I were you," Jed warned.

"Jed, you've been warning me about something ever since I walked in here today. After the sound check, I'll put the drums back the way I found 'em, all right?"

Everyone was so touchy, so nervous about opening for such a big name. We knew we were a good band, a very tight band. All we had to do was run through a

70

forty-five-minute set, turn things over to Dwight and the Hypersensitives, and then drink beer the rest of the night. But I could sense that my bandmates, especially Garth, really wanted to blow away the headline act, the standard dream of every opening band: *Let's show 'em how awesome we are, humiliate 'em, make 'em not even want to come out. Let's play so incredibly well that the crowd demands us back and boos the main act off the stage.*

We did our sound check and got out of the way. In my haste to get some fresh air, I forgot to put the drums back the way I'd found them. I returned to find one of the Yoakam crew readjusting the kit. He spotted me and gave me the evil eye. I began to think Jed was right; maybe I would be killed if I refused to abide by the Yoakam Way.

Soon Bink's began to fill. And fill. And fill. It had never been so crowded. Mac sold as many tickets as he could, paying little attention to the club's limited square footage. But even though the place was horribly overcrowded, he didn't set up chairs on the dance floor because, by God, when people felt like two-stepping, nothing but nothing better stand in their way. Before we went on, Garth assembled us in the Bink's office, where we occasionally met for discussion of such things as purchasing band equipment and future gigs. Garth was wild-eyed, psyched up out of his mind, as if he were getting ready to play the Grand Ole Opry. He got us pumped up, too. I jokingly asked him if we were going to do any of our Yoakam covers.

"Hell, yes," he said. "Only we're gonna do 'em better 'n him."

Everything suddenly had the air of a competition. Our purpose was to *score points* with the audience, *win* them over, *beat* them into submission, *perform* at the peak of our

71

ability, *run* the other band off the stage, *kick* ass. Garth had gone to OSU on a track scholarship, so it was only natural that the competitive fire should spill over into his music. But at this particular show, it became more obvious to us all that when Garth played—whatever he played—he played for keeps.

The bar was a fog of cigarette smoke when Santa Fe took the stage to the applause of our local fans.

"Thanks for comin' out tonight," Garth began. "We're Santa Fe, and we're really glad to be here tonight, playing in front of a guy we all really admire. We're gonna kick it off with a Johnny Cash number that our friend Dwight likes a hell of a lot, too."

Garth called for "Ring of Fire," which Dwight had covered on his album. Within seconds, the dance floor was packed, mostly with people who had been smashed into the back of the bar and needed to breathe. We played a nicely eclectic set: "1982," "Amarillo by Morning," "Sweet Home Alabama," "On the Other Hand," "The Race Is On," Garth's "Much Too Young to Feel This Damn Old," "Great Balls of Fire," "When Will I Be Loved," "Drinking My Baby Goodbye," and, of course, "Old Time Rock 'n Roll." Then, to prepare the crowd for the big show, and to infringe on Dwight's territory just a tad more, we closed with "Guitars and Cadillacs."

The crowd whooped and hollered and made a big fuss and we left the stage feeling like we were really cool. Everyone began to buzz in anticipation of the Yoakam performance. Dwight and his band finally took the stage, squirming their way through the crowd from the kitchen, which served as backstage for such shows. The band tore through all of their hits, plus a couple of obscure Buck Owens numbers that Dwight introduced with religious

72

reverence. Everybody was dancing and singing along and going wild. Dwight's group projected an infectious energy. I noticed the fiddle player the most, an older, bearded guy in his forties wearing a white jumpsuit and a funky, beatnik-style beret. He looked like an old hippie. I asked Mike if the guy was any good, since I didn't understand what differentiated a good fiddler from a great one. Mike smiled, shook his head and just said, "Shoot," meaning, "Hell, yes, he's good! Aincha got any ears?"

If it hadn't been for Dwight's cowboy hat and nasal twang, I wouldn't have thought I was watching a country band at all. They reminded me of Santa Fe, except their sound was a lot cleaner and they were already selling millions of records. Up around the dance floor, Garth stood and swigged a Coke, his eyes glued to the performers onstage. Some of his friends from DuPree Sports were lining up to congratulate him on our set. "Y'all were better than these guys," Garth's friend Raddler told him. "Thanks, Rad," he said, knowing it wasn't true. Garth returned his gaze to the stage, where Dwight was testifying to the new direction of country music. Dwight was very cool in his skin-tight jeans and semi-seductive choreography. Garth seemed to be taking mental notes, watching the faces in the crowd, observing what made them smile, nod their heads, dance, go nuts. After seeing the highly polished Yoakam band, Garth concluded that something still was missing from our sound. The week after the show, he announced that we were going to add another band member, an old friend of his from the Iba Hall athletic dorm.

73

Dale Pierce had been a high-school All-American in the

shot put and discus—a huge, structurally square man whose torso, arms, and legs seemed to be fashioned out of cinder blocks. In between workouts, hours of heaving iron into the next county, he somehow trained his mammoth limbs and digits for the relatively delicate task of playing banjo.

Dale left Woodward, Oklahoma, in the summer of 1979 to bring glory to the orange and black of OSU. One of his first friends in the dorms was a hurdler named Kelly Brooks, Garth's older brother. Kelly walked into Dale's room one day and saw the quiet giant plunking on the banjo and softly singing a bluegrass number.

"My brother plays a little," Kelly said.

"Yeah?" Dale said. "Is he any good?"

Kelly smiled. "He thinks he is."

74   When Garth joined his older brother the next year, he and Dale struck up an instant friendship, borne out of a love of sports and music. Dale introduced Garth to a treasure trove of bluegrass and folk classics. After track practice, Dale, Garth, and Jim Kelley, a graduate-assistant hurdler coach, went back to Iba Hall and entertained themselves and any jocks within earshot.

It was a simple, carefree existence, with only classes and track team duties to interrupt their playing time and dreams of fame and fortune. When they decided they had bored everyone in the dorms with the same old stuff, they took their guitars and banjos and began their assault on the Stillwater public. They first played at Aunt Molly's Amateur Night on Fridays in the Student Union. That started the ball rolling for Garth, who began playing whenever and wherever he could. Sometimes he'd grab Dale and Jim and go over to Stillwater Medical Center to perform in the children's ward. He occasionally played at OSU Posse Club fund-raisers. But the best times were when Garth, Dale, and Jim would just stand out in front of the Student Union at night and jam until a security guard would shoo them back to Iba Hall, where they'd continue crooning until their throats and fingers were raw.

Garth's first steady paying gig was at Ken's Pizza parlor in Midwest City, near his hometown in Yukon. Kelly, Dale, Jim, and another friend of Garth's named Ty England would sometimes go along for the ride, mooch some of Garth's free pizza and, when Garth started running out of tunes, join him onstage for an all-star jock/musician jamboree. When they got back from a show one night, they initiated a pact in Dale's room at Iba Hall.

"We've all gotta swear right now," Dale proclaimed seriously. "Whichever one of us makes it big first has to call the others. Agreed?"

"You better believe it, buddy," said Jim, laughing and giving the big guy an appropriately big slap on the back.

Garth's head bobbed up and down. "I swear I will."

Garth, Jim, and Dale called themselves Dakota Blue. They began writing their own songs and planning a future too sublime to be real. But their fantasies were interrupted by a real tragedy. Jim went flying with a friend one day in a small plane. Shortly after taking off from Stillwater Airport, the plane developed engine trouble and plunged earthward. Jim Kelley was dead.

Dale heard about it first. He went to Garth's room and broke the news. Garth responded by promptly breaking his hand on the nearest door he could find, punching death right in the face. Suddenly nothing mattered. All of his stupid dreams of fame and fortune, glory on the track—

everything seemed so pointless. Had he not smashed his hand, he wouldn't have been able to find any solace in strumming his guitar anyway. It was a time to become introspective, to struggle to make sense of things, to search for the reason why God had suddenly decided to put the whole world on automatic pilot.

5

The Stillwater Circuit

By the time Garth talked to Dale about joining Santa Fe, Dale had learned how to play the Dobro, an instrument that looks like a guitar with a hubcap glued on top. But it was not Dale's banjo or Dobro expertise Garth sought; he wanted Dale to play the pedal steel guitar. Dale had tinkered with the steel but had two main reservations about pursuing it further: it is difficult to master—its tuning scheme is entirely different than that of the guitar or Dobro—and it is a confining instrument. Dale simply detested the idea of sitting on his duff in front of an audience. As he told Garth, "If I have to sit for four hours, I'd better have a steering wheel in front of me."

Still, Garth was so confident that Dale would change his mind that he asked Dale to come to the band's first photo session, which Garth arranged one Saturday afternoon at a place across the street from Bink's called Candids 'n Casuals. Garth wore his stiffest, starchiest shirt and a white

Stetson. Jed donned a red neckerchief, shiny black boots, and a tan, Western-style shirt that would've looked pretty spiffy back in the 1930s. The rest of us wore whatever wasn't too dirty. The photographer had us goof around and act as if we were having the best of times. Even though I had grown fond of the guys in the band, I found it difficult to pretend I was overjoyed about playing country music; I remained convinced that it was doing irreparable damage to my musical sensibility.

While we were setting up at Bink's the following weekend, Garth came in with a packet of proofs from the photo session. At least half of the pictures were rendered useless because of my stupid facial expressions and rude gestures, which were my crude way of demonstrating my antipathy to country music. Garth said nothing but I could tell he was steamed. In trying to distance myself from country, I had succeeded only in disappointing friends and looking like a jerk. I was terribly embarrassed, but it gave me the healthy and long-overdue attitude adjustment I needed.

Had I had my head on straight from the beginning, I would have seen that Santa Fe had become exactly what Garth had promised: a band that played country, not a country band. Garth knew we couldn't survive two weeks at Bink's or anywhere else in Stillwater just playing George Jones and Johnny Cash. That was why he kept our repertoire well stocked with Bob Seger, Steve Miller, and Eagles classics. We even played current pop hits by Huey Lewis, Dire Straits, Bruce Springsteen, and John Cougar or John Cougar Mellencamp or whatever he called himself then.

Occasionally we overstepped our capabilities, like when Garth decided we should cover a big hit by the Outfield called "Your Love." The song features some inhumanly high-pitched vocals that forced Garth to sing with the posture of a weightlifter preparing to press four hundred pounds, and Tom and Mike practically had to levitate to hit the harmonies. When Garth noticed the rest of us sighing in unison every time "Your Love" came up, he scratched it off the list. But it was all part of Garth's plan for Santa Fe to be all things to all people, and for the most part we were succeeding. We were playing somewhere every weekend, and Mac made sure we opened for all of the big acts he assembled at Bink's that summer: Johnny Paycheck, the New Grass Revival, Becky Hobbs, Steve Earle, and Pake McEntire, Reba's little brother. Bink's was comfortable; it was home. But, like a kid who gets tired of living with parents, we began to sense that it was time to move away from our secure environment. And we could not have chosen a less secure set of circumstances than one particular evening at the Sundowner.

Garth got word that a traveling guitarist and his female singing partner were touring the country and using local bands for backup. Being the most pliable group in the area, we were chosen for the honor. Since the gig was to be at the Sundowner, all of us made sure we stayed outside as long as possible before showtime to inhale all the fresh air we could. Because once inside Honky-Tonk Hell, one abandoned all hope of breathing any oxygen that had not already been sucked through a Marlboro filter.

After setting up the equipment, we went backstage to meet the bandleaders for the night, the incomparable Jack Boles and his lovely sidekick, Becky Baker. Jack was probably fifty-five but looked more like seventy, with slick white hair, a big, bulbous honker, and a face that seemed to be chiseled out of red Oklahoma clay.

One of the usable photos from the band's first photo session, June 1986. *Top:* Jed, Mike, Dale. *Bottom:* Matt, Garth, Tom. Photo by Paul House.

"*Hell*-o, there, fellas," Jack boomed, offering his big clammy hand to everyone. "Heard a *lot* about you boys. Unnerstand you all can really *pick*. I want you to meet a real sweetheart who can really sing her tail off—Becky Baker." Jack had one of those loud speaking voices that theater actors develop from *projecting* all the time. He commanded our attention like a marines drill instructor.

"H'lo, boys," Becky said with a delicious southern drawl.

"So, Mr. Boles," Garth said ever so politely, "what're we gonna play tonight?"

"Jack, son. Call me Jack. Mr. Boles was my father," said the son of Mr. Boles. Jack fired off a list of songs, which could have been from the Tin Pan Alley days for all I knew. Garth, Mike, and Tom nodded their heads at the mention of a few tunes, but more often they looked at one another with confused expressions. "Y'all just watch me for the keys and the breaks, and we'll get through this just *fine*," Jack assured us.

They were a pair, Becky and Jack. Becky looked to be in her late early forties. She was tall, very pretty, with a big head of unruly brunette hair and a warm, sensual personality. She had full lips and hips and blinding white teeth. From what we could gather, she had had a big hit at one time, and Jack had decided to take her under his wing and promote her. Jack told us he had played for Roy Clark and some other Nashville icons way back when. None of us had any reason to doubt his word, so we were intrigued to play with someone with such experience. Pretty soon it was showtime, and we assembled onstage for the biggest musical pop quiz of our lives. No sooner had we got into position than Jack whirled around and spouted, "This one's in D, boys, and it goes a one, a two, a you know what to do . . ."

Jack, with his guitar cranked up near jet-engine level, launched himself and Becky into a song for which we were all completely unprepared. The real musicians caught on soon enough, but I felt as though I was at the beginning of a race with my shoes untied. Jack's guitar was so loud I couldn't figure out his rhythm, and Tom and Garth were concentrating so hard that they didn't realize I wasn't even near the beat I was supposed to be playing. Mike inconspicuously turned down the volume on his fiddle and pretended he was in control while Jed's left hand raced around the guitar neck, stabbing at chords.

And so the night went, with each song a new experience in mind reading and mind bending. "This little booger starts in G and we go to A after the bridge. Now hold on tight, boys. A three, a four, now open up the *door* . . ."

Jack was in his own world, shouting his incomprehensible cadence, occasionally coming out of the clouds to belch some harmony or deliver an earsplitting lead on his Fender. I caught Jed's eyes during one of Jack's solos. It was obvious what at least one guy onstage was thinking: "God *damn* he's loud!"

Despite every ragged beginning, every off note, and every train-wreck ending, the crowd didn't appear to think anything was awry onstage. It was an older crowd, mostly men who probably ended every day at the Downer. Most were genuinely glad just to see someone the likes and looks of Becky Baker performing in such a dive. After the set, if it can truly be called that, Jack gave me his sweaty red neckerchief as a reward for having endured such a fiasco, and Becky autographed posters for all of us.

Santa Fe proper took the stage again. Still reeling from the absurd Jack Boles showcase, we needed several songs to get back into the swing of things. After the show, Jack and Becky bade us farewell and continued their tour of small towns across the land, no doubt befuddling every band they lured into their musical maelstrom. In later shows, in a fond tribute to our animated, enigmatic friend, Garth and Tom occasionally kicked off songs with "A one, a two, a you know what to do." And for a split second the memory of Jack Boles returned, and with it the peculiar feeling of waking up in a cold sweat from a bad dream in a stranger's house in a foreign country.

Aching for fresh air and elbow room, Garth called upon

his legion of connections to get us booked at Stillwater's two gigantic dance halls, Tumbleweed and the Cimarron Country Ballroom, where the serious boot-scooters congregated to revel in that indoor country-fair ambience. You had to be a dedicated two-stepper to drive all the way to these places, particularly the Weed, which in those days required miles of unlit, bumpy dirt-road navigation through scores of notoriously perilous intersections. Around campus on Mondays, it was easy to tell which trucks and cars had been guided to the Weed over the weekend. The sure signs were the mud-caked headlights, taillights, tires, and quarter panels. Another giveaway was little nicks in the windshield caused by flying gravel. The third and perhaps most obvious indicator was the truck bed full of empty beer and Skoal cans.

To a certain breed of OSU student, Friday and Saturday nights meant squeezing into Wranglers, sliding on Tony Llamas, stuffing in a wad of snuff, and making the long dusty trek to Tumbleweed, about seven miles west of campus. The handful of true cowboys who roamed the plains of the OSU campus—OSU has a Future Farmers of America fraternity—made a pilgrimage to the Weed every week. Most of the Tumbleweed crowd, however, consisted of the weekend goat-roper set, those who wore tennis shoes and Ralph Lauren shirts to class during the week and then magically transformed into Roy or Dale Rogers at precisely 8:00 P.M. on Friday. It was a crowd similar to that at Bink's but with a rougher edge, thanks to the influx of rowdies from nearby blue-collar towns such as Perry and Morrison, where people sweated their asses off at the factory or the feed store all week and thus felt entitled to blow off a little steam by hittin' the Weed and

83

mixin' with them college-goin' sissies.

To Garth, playing Tumbleweed was like going home. He felt a huge sense of pride in bringing his own band to the fore and serving as the Weed's master of ceremonies, when only months earlier he had been just another of its underpaid and underappreciated ushers. Things were looking up for Garth Brooks. Indeed, it became apparent that summer of 1986 that the band was really Garth Brooks and Santa Fe. In July, a story about the band appeared on the front page of the *Stillwater NewsPress* entertainment section, with a big picture of Garth playing his guitar. In the article, Garth talked a little about his musical heritage, how once he had been offered a chance to play with Opryland USA but turned it down (which none of us knew about until we read the story), why he thought the music business "sucks," and why he thought Santa Fe was "one of the hottest sounds around." It was nice press for the band, but the article strongly implied that it was Garth the people came to see.

This was no secret to anyone who came to one of our shows, and certainly not to the group itself, as gig protocol would suggest. In between sets, Garth usually went out into the crowd to schmooze with his adoring public while the rest of Santa Fe retreated to the parking lot for a smoke and to hear Tom and Mike tell the latest jokes circulating around the Stillwater post office. Personally, as soon as I crashed the set's last cymbal, I couldn't wait to get outside, stare at the sky, and turn off my brain. Even though we had been at it only a few months, the romance of playing in one of the town's most popular bands had begun to wear off. Playing became work. Sometimes it was downright drudgery, especially those occasional four-night gigs at Bink's and the Sundowner.

It was even physically painful. Since musicians don't keep the most regular hours, at any given time one of us was fighting a cold or some other ailment. There were times when I honestly wondered if Tom was going to live much longer because of the awful chest colds he got, which made him cough so loudly that he'd drown out Garth, yet he persisted with his steady diet of coffee and Salems. And even though it appears that drummers have it easy because they sit down all evening, one should never discount their susceptibility to certain ailments. Between gigs and practices, I usually logged an average of thirty hours per week squirming around on a small, rock-hard drum stool. By the end of that summer with Santa Fe, I was forced to begin using a device known among medical professionals as an invalid cushion and more widely as a doughnut. Before the first song of each set, I discreetly inflated my IC and, with a grimace, gingerly situated my tender rear upon it. The guys in the band had a lot of fun with my agony. I don't remember if anyone in the audience ever razzed me, nor would I have cared if they did. No degree of embarrassment could have made me exchange comfort for pride.

Garth, on the other hand, seemed to recharge his batteries with every show. He couldn't get enough of performing. When he wasn't performing, he was looking forward to the next performance. While the rest of us were suffering through plagues and having problems most people aren't bothered with until they're old geezers, Garth was burning with music fever like no one I had ever seen. Even at that early stage of the band's career, we all began to sense that he would probably one day

Garth in the *Stillwater NewsPress* newsroom, when he was interviewed for an article published in the summer of 1986. Photo credit: *Stillwater NewsPress*.

enjoy some degree of national success, with or without the rest of us.

He was certainly in prime physical and mental form at Tumbleweed that weekend. It helped that we were finally on a real stage where the standing musicians could spread out and not fear jabbing someone in the Adam's apple whenever they made a sudden move. Garth made full use of the wide open spaces, covering a good two or three miles up and down the promenade while delivering his musical sermon. It was an unquestionable triumph for Garth, the athlete-cum-performer, who capitalized on his home-field advantage.

Whereas Tumbleweed was mostly frequented by the young, the Cimarron Country Ballroom—located about seven miles south of town, halfway between Stillwater and the neighboring hamlet of Perkins—attracted a more genteel group: retired cattlemen, businessmen, Freemasons with their boisterous laughs and strange handshakes, middle-aged divorcées looking for action, and the many salvage-yard owners who operated in that part of the county. On any given night at the Cimarron, nearly everyone knew everyone, and everyone without exception knew the club's owner, because it's impossible not to become friends instantly with a man named Buck Dollarhide.

Buck is a man as big and outgoing as his name suggests. He drove the biggest pickup imaginable, wore the biggest belt buckle and biggest Stetson, and operated the biggest damned ballroom around. And because Buck knew how to pick a guitar and belt out a tune, he naturally built one hell of a big stage for his bands, and for himself, to play on. Buck always made the rounds in the audience, making sure everyone was having a good time and that no one was

Tumbleweed, looking appropriately desolate. This was the scene of two of Garth's greatest triumphs: headlining at the club where he used to bounce drunks, and, of course, his first encounter with Sandy. Photo by the author.

88

getting too rambunctious. But usually by the third set, the urge to get up and jam with the band overwhelmed him, spiriting him away from his duties as host. As soon as we saw Buck shuffling toward the stage with that big guitar in his hand and that look in his eyes, we knew it was time to waltz. Buck played them all: "Tennessee Waltz," "Missouri Waltz," and all those other standards in three-four time that sound exactly the same except for the name of the state. But because Buck treated us so well, we didn't mind playing whatever he wanted.

Nothing ever went wrong at the Cimarron. The crowds were always extremely receptive, the sound mix always superb, and the complimentary beverages always rejuvenating. Santa Fe got spoiled on that big stage, six feet off the ground, playing for happy, romantic audiences who looked up and smiled at us as they waltzed past, and who actually made the effort to clap when songs were over. The Cimarron never had a crowd we had to "work." They were always easy, as easy as playing a waltz with Buck Dollarhide.

After one such pleasant Saturday evening in August of 1986—after piling my drums into my '67 Chrysler Newport, after waiting for Garth to materialize from Buck's office with my share of the weekend's haul, after stopping at the Buy 'n Bye for a cup of coffee, scanning my AM radio for a late-night talk show, hopping on lonely Highway 51 East to Tulsa, and inviting the warm wind to blow the sweat and smoke off my body—I admitted to myself for the first time that I liked playing country music. At least I did with Garth, Tom, Jed, and Mike. To my surprise, playing country was molding me into a very good drummer because country music demands a solid beat-keeper, unlike the frantic rock bands I'd been in. And back then, when my priorities were so simple they were practically imbecilic, to know that I was a good drummer in a good band was as important as knowing my parents loved me.

With summer drawing to a close, it was time to decide if I should return for my *seventh* year of college or answer the inexorable call of reality. But this time my decision was not weighted with the guilt of mooching money from my father, since the band was playing regularly enough to afford me the tuition and meager room and board of a typical collegian. I decided that I would go to OSU for one more year, get a teaching certificate in secondary education, play in the band until its inevitable demise, then return to Tulsa to make my fortune as a high-school English teacher.

Meanwhile, Garth was making plans of his own—for himself and for the rest of the band.

6

On the Road with Santa Fe

Even with the band playing every weekend and sometimes
four or five times a week, Garth stuck to his Wednesday
night solo routine at Willie's. With the fall semester beginning, he felt it was high time to show off his group to
his faithful followers, give them a dose of electric Garth.
After enjoying the spacious platforms of the Weed and
the Cimarron all summer, playing on Willie's toy stage
was like visiting our old grade school and trying to squeeze
into our old desks. But it was exciting because even though
we'd been a group for five months, we hadn't yet played
the Strip, the heart of campus life.

To help us sound more professional, Garth hired Johnny
Wright to coordinate all of our sound equipment. An off-
beat, extremely intelligent, and brutally frank fellow with
straight black hair down to his shoulder blades, Johnny
was a local mandolin picker and former bandmate of the
Skinners. His first challenge was to keep us from blowing

The Strip, with Edmon Low library in the background. Photo by the author.

92

out everyone's ears at Willie's, not an easy task in a bar with such limited square footage and odd dimensions. Johnny commandeered a booth next to the stage for his huge mixing board, which was appropriate for a big place like Tumbleweed but overkill for Willie's. He shoehorned as much equipment onstage as he could. But there wasn't enough room for the extra guitars and Garth's two little Peavey PA speakers, so he placed them directly in front of the stage, which happened to be the only designated place in the bar to dance. Because it was Garth's home court, Willie's was packed beyond capacity for both shows, which was great for beer sales but bad for any unprotected musical instruments. Too many times to count, dancers got too close to the stage and knocked guitars off their stands into a heap, to the horror of Tom and Jed. Drunken butts swerved out of control and bumped into the two

PA speakers, making them wobble perilously atop their stands, but to our amazement neither fell. Garth had no room to do his usual gyrating. He simply had to sing and play and try not to get distracted by the leaning towers of Peavey. Over in his cramped sound booth, Johnny was going completely nuts worrying about the equipment, but he managed to give us an excellent mix. The atmosphere at Willie's was so claustrophobic that even Garth stepped out to join us for some air between sets.

"How would you boys like to get the hell out of this place?" Garth asked after we assembled in the parking lot.

"But we've got two more sets to do," I naively replied.

Garth smiled. "No, man, I don't mean Willie's. I'm talkin' about this town, this state. Guys, we've gotta start thinking about Nashville."

Silence.

"*Moving* to Nashville."

93

More silence as each began contemplating the idea. Off and on, Garth had mentioned trying Nashville again, but we knew he was serious this time. Nobody said yes, nobody said no.

"When?" asked Mike.

Garth shrugged his shoulders, leaned back against a truck, and looked up at the stars. "What the hell are we waitin' for?"

To get the band used to the idea of traveling and playing, Garth lined up gigs around the state. Our first big out-of-town date was in mid-September at Tulsa's most popular honky-tonk, Tulsa City Limits. The OSU–University of Tulsa football game was to be played the same weekend in Tulsa, and since OSU–TU is a huge rivalry, Garth knew thousands of OSU students would be traveling to the game. We advertised our show in the *Daily O'Collegian*, the campus newspaper, and hit the stage Friday night greeted by about two hundred or so game-crazed OSU fans. To the Tulsa City Limits management, it looked as if we had a massive following.

Tulsa City Limits is as big as Tumbleweed and the Cimarron Ballroom, but doesn't have the rustic charm of the other two. It's a modern country bar, built at the height of the *Urban Cowboy* craze, with groovy neon lights, the latest video games, and a big fiberglass '55 Chevy hanging over its enormous dance floor. Take away the cowboy hats and you'd have Disco City Limits. For bands, one of the club's most appealing features is an offstage dressing room, something we weren't accustomed to. Even though it was pretty grungy—dark and dank, with a couple of garage-sale couches, wobbly tables, and a small bathroom—it was private space, which is exactly what every band needs to prepare itself physically and mentally for each performance. That is, it was a place to wolf down some McDonald's, have a brew, rehearse songs, and invite your friends to impress them with what *really* goes on backstage, which is nothing at all. Best of all, having a dressing room meant not having to wait in line for the public john and not having to duck outside to the parking lot to avoid the ubiquitous Lynyrd Skynyrd freaks who corner you to ask, "You guys know 'Freebird?'" No crowd contact for us, baby. All we had to do was play on our six-feet-off-the-floor stage, towering above our audience like musical gods, then disappear to our safe haven.

The shows at Tulsa City Limits were as successful as could be. We never played better and the crowds were big both nights, thanks to the OSU crew. Garth had a

94

mini-reunion with some of his old playing buddies that weekend. Ty England stopped by on Friday night and joined us for a set. Garth's sister, Betsy Smittle, sat in with us on Saturday night and sang "Me and Bobby McGee" and a few other songs. Betsy at the time was playing in local star Gus Hardin's band. After hearing her wail and play, I realized Garth's family must have a gigantic performance gene in its DNA. She played as though she'd been fronting our band for years. Jed responded to Betsy's show-stopping voice by unleashing the rock'n roll demons in his fingers, playing solos that had everyone in the club shaking their heads in wonder. Of all the guys in Santa Fe, Jed got noticeably better with each show. I know I've never seen or played with a better guitarist. He could play so sweetly and softly one moment, so savagely the next. I spent a lot of time during shows listening to Jed. He was the main reason I became a more conservative drummer; trampling on one of his licks was a musical mortal sin.

After Saturday's show, the Tulsa City Limits management asked us back to play during the International Finals Rodeo in mid-January, a real coup since that was usually the biggest week of the year for the club. Garth was ecstatic.

We spent the next two weekends at Bink's getting grooved for the Marlboro Talent Roundup semifinals on October 8 in Tuttle, Oklahoma, a dust mite on the map just outside Oklahoma City. The contest was to be held at a small indoor rodeo arena called Jamie D's. The winner moved on to the finals to compete for five thousand dollars and a chance to open for Merle Haggard, Ricky Skaggs, and the Judds at the Myriad in Oklahoma City later in the month. The rules were simple: give it everything you had in ten minutes or less—but not a second more or you were disqualified—then await the decision of the judges, who scored on showmanship, tightness of performance, crowd appeal, and other completely subjective categories.

A band contest is like a musical gymnastics meet. Every second of the performance is critical. Any bad notes, dropped drumsticks, or clumsy endings would mean we could kiss our chance at five thousand big ones goodbye. We rehearsed our ten-minute performance at Tom's house. Over and over we practiced shortened versions of four of our standards. Garth asked Tom to sing Steve Earle's "Guitar Town" as one of the numbers, mostly for variety's sake but probably also to reassure us that we were still a group, not a solo guy with a backup band. Since Garth played bass on the song, he and Tom rehearsed exchanging guitars like two relay runners practicing their baton handoff.

Band contests are also mind games. When we arrived, we saw about fourteen other bands milling around in their spangling shirts and cowboy hats and ropers and Wranglers, all freshly pressed and starched to the hilt, strutting their star quality. Most of the guys looked like characters right out of a Marlboro ad—a strategy to woo the judges, perhaps—but one group wore black leather and tattoos, with long, stringy hair and permanent snarls. It was the first time I'd ever seen cowpunks. They intimidated me more than all of the George Strait clones. I figured that if they didn't win the contest, they would probably be given a prize for Most Likely to Knife an Audience Member.

We were third on the bill. About fifteen Stillwater groupies made the trip to support us, including Raddler and his sister Jana Shipley—who probably came to more of our shows than anyone else, even Sandy—and some DuPree Sports faithful. They helped keep us relaxed, but as it got closer to our turn, we started getting nervous.

"We're not doing the third verse on 'Diggin' Up Bones,' right?"

"Right. Remember, we're going into the chorus after the lead."

"Is the lead after the bridge?"

"There's no bridge on 'Diggin' Up Bones.' "

"What if I throw up?"

"I don't care. Just keep playing."

The first couple of groups were pretty good, but we knew we could blow 'em off the stage. And we did. We opened with George Strait's "Unwound," mellowed out a little with Randy Travis's "Diggin' Up Bones," made the guitar switch and sailed through "Guitar Town," then passed the baton back and went home with Dwight Yoakam's "Guitars and Cadillacs." All, as they say, without a hitch.

97

The Stillwater contingent led the cheers, and we knew we had the early lead. We hustled our instruments and sweaty armpits offstage, relieved it was over, and sat down with our fans to watch the rest of the groups try to knock us off the mountain. At least seven groups did George Strait's "Nobody in His Right Mind," which at that time was high on the country charts. After hearing it for the fourth time, though, we thought no band in its right mind would perform the song again. But each band had its ten minutes rehearsed so precisely that improvising a different number could've spelled doom. So we heard it again. And again. One poor fellow did a lackluster solo routine, nerves having stripped him of any stage presence he may have had. Our hearts went out to him, especially when he closed with "Nobody in His Right Mind."

But neither our sympathy nor our cockiness lasted long. The cowpunks, all gloom and attitude, took the stage next and completely tore the place apart, the highlight of their performance a particularly evil version of Charlie Daniels's "The Devil Went Down to Georgia." The group's fiddle player looked like Edgar Winter with a cowboy hat: thin as a reed, neon-white skin, with spider webs and ghouls and other demonic images tattooed all over his arms. But he could skin that fiddle alive, and the crowd, either because they were hypnotized or scared out of their minds, went wild.

Because we thought the Marlboro people were looking for traditional acts, and because the cowpunks were about as traditional country as Deep Purple, we convinced ourselves they weren't a threat. But a couple of bands later, a group that sounded one hell of a lot like Santa Fe took the stage and ended our speculation about who would win the contest. They were slightly more polished than we were, far more wholesome looking—every damn one of them looked like George Strait—and generally the kind of crowd-pleasing folks who win such contests. After they were awarded first place, one of the judges told us we had placed third on the ballot. We assumed the cowpunks had taken second, and were thankful we weren't the ones who had to tell them.

Our blindly loyal fans scoffed at the decision, told us we were by far the best, and actually had us believing they were right. Good sports Tom and Garth went over to the winning band, congratulated them, and wished them luck

98

Santa Fe on campus, performing on a trailer bed just to the east of OSU's Old Central Library, July 1986. Photo by Kevin Maloney.

in the finals. Jed, Mike, and I went to buy a beer to cel-ebrate the whole thing being over. Garth seemed rather subdued afterward, more disappointed than any of us that we hadn't won.

At that point, we were a good, solid band, but there was nothing unbelievably fantastic about us. We could play an entire evening without any screwups, which is more than a lot of seasoned bands could say, but there was nothing to indicate that we had the potential to draw an enormous au-dience. Except for "Much Too Young to Feel This Damn Old," we played covers; we were a good dance/cover band. We had been playing for nearly seven months and we were getting better with each performance, but Garth knew we had a lot to prove before the Nashville move could be justified. Losing the Marlboro contest gave Garth a nec-essary dose of reality. So, in order to assess just how good the band was, he decided to see how we'd fare in a place where absolutely nobody had ever heard of us.

Someone associated with one of Garth's OSU Posse Club friends arranged for us to play at New Mexico State University's alumni reunion in Las Cruces, just north of the Mexican border. Two weeks after the Marlboro contest, on a radiant Thursday evening in late October, we found ourselves heading south with the birds for what would be one of the most memorable but exhausting weekends in Santa Fe history.

We left Stillwater around sundown and stopped off at Garth's parents' house in Yukon for a feed of mammoth proportions. Garth's mother prepared a gigantic bowl of potato salad and an ocean of beans and slaw and what seemed like half a cow's worth of hamburgers. Garth's brother Kelly was there to send us off and to help scarf everything down. It was Oklahoma hospitality at its finest and Mrs. Brooks was the ultimate hostess, encouraging all of us to eat until we were moaning like gorged heifers. After two hours of gluttony, it was time to begin the long haul to Las Cruces. Jed, Tom, and I crammed ourselves into Jed's SuperCab and Garth and Mike boarded the Jimmy. We drove in the dark, down through southwest Oklahoma, through the panhandle of Texas, passing through Amarillo by very early morning, drinking coffee and watching millions of little white lines pass by.

"Jed, you want me to drive for a while?" I asked.

"Naw, I'm fine."

We were running out of things to talk about when we passed through a little town in Texas called Bovina. When we saw a huge grain silo with "Bovina" written in gigantic letters, Jed and Tom were for some reason overcome by a fit of insane laughter. Bovina jokes and Bovina songs and images of a small-town Texas gal named Bovina Regina Cowsill kept us occupied until Roswell, when we decided to find alternative entertainment on the radio. It was around 3:00 A.M. and we were getting a little bleary-eyed. We found a station that seemed to play Marty Robbins every other song, setting the mood for our expedition into this mysteriously beautiful state, aptly named Land of Enchantment. As Marty sang "A White Sport Coat and a Pink Carnation," I recalled my special fondness for New Mexico. My father spent a lot of time painting the secluded adobe villages there, and it was in Santa Fe that I had my first déjà vu experience. I was nine years old when Dad took us there for a vacation. We visited an art gallery where some of his pictures hung. The moment I walked into the gallery I realized I knew where everything was. It was as though I had visited it a hundred times before. I had no idea what déjà vu was, had never even heard of the phenomenon, so I was naturally a little perplexed, and at one point thought I was getting ready to die. But at the same time I was fascinated by the experience. Before going into each room in the gallery, I told myself exactly what I was going to see: "In this next room will be a bronze of an Indian on a horse, a painting of a mountain scene with sheep in the foreground, and some relics of Indian warriors—shields and bows and tomahawks and stuff." And there everything would be, just as I had seen it in my mind. But so far, all we had seen of New Mexico on this trip was darkness and the occasional city lights way off on the horizon.

101

"Jed, you want me to drive now?" one of us would ask between yawns.

"Naw, I'm OK."

While we were writing songs about cowgirls and reminiscing about past visits, over in the other half of the convoy Garth and Mike were talking about the future.

"You know what, Mike?" Garth said just before we hit Alamogordo.

"Whassat?" Mike replied, snapping out of a half-sleep.

Garth adjusted himself in his seat and hunched over the steering wheel like a kid getting ready for his first roller-coaster ride. "I'm going to be bigger than Hank Williams."

Mike wondered if he were really awake. "Is that right?" he asked with feigned interest.

"Hank Williams *Senior*," Garth added.

Mike, still not convinced he was awake, turned his head toward the crazy man guiding them down the dark highway. "How're you gonna do that?"

Garth laughed. "Man," he said, "I'm *doin'* it!"

Mike realized that anyone whose head was reeling with such wild notions wasn't likely to fall asleep at the wheel any time soon. So while Garth continued to lay out his plans aloud, Mike relaxed and drifted away, sleeping through one of the most interesting secrets he or anyone could ever want to hear.

Back in our truck, no one was sleeping. I find it impossible to sleep in a moving vehicle, no matter how tired I am. With all the nicotine and caffeine in Tom's system, sleep was out of the question. But Tom and I were worried Jed might start to drift off. He had been piloting the truck for eleven hours straight, and we asked him over and over if we could relieve him, if for no other reason than to do something besides sit on our sore butts.

102

"How many times do I have to tell you guys I'm all right?"

"C'mon, Jed," I pleaded, "why don't you take a break? I won't wreck your truck. I've driven bigger clunkers than this rig." I was lying; nothing was bigger than that monstrous SuperCab.

"Forget it," he said, ending the conversation.

Just outside Alamogordo, the sun started to come up. After being surrounded by darkness for hours on end, suddenly we found ourselves facing the magnificent San Andres Mountains in a perfect New Mexican dawn. Oklahomans aren't accustomed to seeing mountains, so all of us were momentarily charged with energy. But with the sunlight Jed realized that he had been staring at the road way too long.

"I'm pulling over," said Jed. "I'm seeing double."

He honked the horn and flashed his lights to get Garth to pull over. Tom took the wheel and we resumed our journey, slicing through the mountain range into Las Cruces. Oklahomans also aren't accustomed to seeing military installations in the middle of the desert, and we gawked at the unsettling sight of the White Sands Missile Range.

"Hell of a place for a gig," I remarked. "Right, Jed?" But our cross-eyed captain was asleep as soon as he took his hands off the wheel.

The first thing we noticed about Las Cruces was how unbelievably clean it was; *barren* may be a more appropriate word. Our second observation was that there were no buildings over six stories tall. And everything adobe, as though it grew right out of the earth.

We found our motel and Garth went in to the front desk and got the keys to our rooms. We unloaded our

103

travel bags and went straight to the hotel restaurant, where we piled pancakes and sausage and coffee on top of the big glob of dough and beef and beans still sitting in our stomachs from the night before, which at that point seemed more like weeks before. We ate in silence like monks, our forks and spoons clinking and clanging on our plates against the backdrop of traditional motel-restaurant Muzak. Occasionally someone would utter, "Pass the jelly," or "Ma'am, can we have some more coffee over here?" We finished breakfast around eight, stepped outside into the cool fall air, yawned, burped, and wiped the cheese out of our eyes. For about ten minutes we just stared at the San Andres Mountains, which helped confirm that the last fourteen hours had not been a dream. It was a cloudless day, the sky so blue it was almost purple. Our first performance was on the NMSU campus at noon, so we went back to the rooms to relax. If we'd had any sense we would have taken naps, but that probably would have made us feel even more tired. Instead we all took showers and drank yet more coffee to revive ourselves.

104

We were to play two shows: that afternoon in front of the Student Union and the next night in the main Student Union auditorium. After cleaning up and staring at the TV for an hour, we drove to the campus, hopped a curb, and drove along the sidewalk up to the stage in front of the Student Union, getting dirty looks from the students we scooted out of the way. Stapled on a pole beside the stage was a flyer advertising our band. There was a picture of us, the name of our band, and a quote:

"Really Gets 'em Dancin'."
— Buck Dollarhide, owner of the Cimarron Country Ballroom, Stillwater, OK

Big Buck had followed us all the way to Las Cruces to give us a plug. As we set up our gear, though, we weren't thinking about whether or not we could really get the New Mexico folks dancin'; we were concerned about being able to stay awake long enough to play at all.

A short, chubby Hispanic kid about eighteen years old came up and introduced himself. His name was Sonny. I don't know where he came from or if he was part of the alumni association, but he somehow became our roadie for the weekend. He helped us unload our equipment, ran our wires all over the place, and brought us drinks. Sonny had dark, bloodshot eyes that didn't fit his youthful face. He was a real fireball, and all he ever talked about was a town called Juarez.

"You guys going down to Juarez tonight?" Sonny asked.

"Where?" we asked.

"Juarez," he repeated. With Sonny's breathy Mexican accent, it sounded as if he was saying "Wharz."

"What's in *Wharz*?" Jed asked.

"Oh, man, *every*thing. You know." Then he just smiled in that devilishly boyish way that meant "sex, booze, drugs, and general mayhem."

"I don't know, Sonny," Jed replied. "We'll have to see how we feel. We're pretty tired."

"Oh, man," said Sonny, "you gotta go to Juarez. You won't believe it."

In junior college, I'd heard the legend of Boystown, some place just over the Mexican border that supposedly made Sodom and Gomorrah seem like a church retreat. Some of my friends claimed to have gone there on spring break and returned with all sense of innocence permanently erased. The way Sonny talked, I began to believe that Ciudad Juarez and Boystown were one and the same.

"Where is *Wharz*?" Tom asked, noticeably amused by our mischievous roadie.

"It's about thirty minutes from here," Sonny said, followed by a momentary pause when his dark eyes suddenly opened wide. "In Mexico (*May-he-co*)."

"We'll think about it," Jed said. Being the certified paranoiac I was, I knew I wasn't going anywhere near *Wharz*.

As we did our sound check, some older alums started sitting down in the fifty or so metal folding chairs in front of the stage. By around noon, twenty or thirty people, mostly in their forties or older, had positioned themselves to check us out. Garth surveyed the scene and decided to wake everyone up with "Drinking My Baby Goodbye."

After Garth introduced us, we blasted into the song. We hoped the students passing by would make a detour and rush over, blow off their afternoon classes, and come get into our good vibes. Some of the students in the dormitory across from the Student Union leaned out of the windows and then quickly disappeared. A few others on the way to class stopped to watch. A man driving a horse and carriage, probably one of the weekend's homecoming attractions, came loping up the sidewalk and parked by the bandstand.

> So pour me another one
> I'm finished with the other one
> I'm drinkin' my baby g'bye.

We concluded our first song on New Mexico soil and were greeted by—absolutely nothing. I cannot exaggerate the lack of response. It was as though during the course

106

of the song someone had replaced our audience members with cardboard cutouts. Or as though they were watching TV in their living rooms and felt it pointless to applaud. The blank looks on their faces were so ridiculous that all of us, even Garth, busted out laughing. Even then the audience refused to so much as blink. It was so absurd that we momentarily believed that this whole trip had indeed been a dream. Then, as the exclamation point to our audience's apathy, the horse standing next to the bandstand suddenly released a waterfall of urine on the sidewalk. And what an impressive stream it was, ricocheting off the concrete as loudly as a string of Black Cats. *That* the people noticed, as did the five delirious members of Santa Fe. On and on it flowed, for a full minute or more. We couldn't help but marvel at the tremendous output. As the pungent smell of horse pee wafted across the stage, Tom recalled Buck Dollarhide's eloquent tribute: "Santa Fe," he snickered. "Really gets 'em pissin'."

107

We played our hearts out while the sleepy students cruised by and the audience members swayed almost imperceptibly in their seats. To be fair, it was a little early in the day to get people fired up about doing the boogie-woogie. The absence of alcohol and the serene, hypnotically beautiful weather probably had much to do with the trance everyone seemed to be in. Still, it was discouraging to have come so far to receive such a blasé reception. We piled the gear into the trucks and headed back to the hotel.

That night we went into town to check out the scene. We ended up at a honky-tonk near our motel, had a few beers, shot a little pool, and watched a pretty good band cover every song we ever did. We realized we were as bored and detached as the rest of the zombies in the bar, and began to wonder why in the hell we were out looking for entertainment when we were so exhausted and mentally flaccid from our innocuous afternoon gig.

"Maybe we should've gone down to *Wharz* with Sonny," Jed joked. At that point, our bodies were trying desperately to metabolize all the caffeine, nicotine, alcohol, and heavy food in our systems, and the severe lack of sleep wasn't helping matters. As a result, we all felt as silly and helpless as teenagers at an Everclear punch party. The simple act of using the word *Juarez* in every sentence suddenly became the funniest thing in the world. We did that for about half an hour. We were crying we were laughing so hard. Everyone in the bar looked at us and probably assumed we had just tried pot for the first time. As soon as we realized how ridiculous all this was, we got up and left. It was only ten o'clock when we returned to the motel. We watched the news and finally gave in to what our bodies had been craving for twenty-four hours.

Weather-wise, the next day was like the first: perfect. But it wasn't warm enough to swim at the motel pool in the courtyard, and the little miniature golf course next to the pool was closed for repairs. So Mike, Jed, and I did what most bored traveling musicians do: we got some beer and went back to the motel. Jed sat in a corner with his guitar and played any song we requested, astounding us with his infinite library of licks. We watched a football game on TV. We read the paper. No one had any desire to go driving around. Jed was by far the most traveled musician of the band, so he was a pro at sitting on his duff. We began to get a taste of what it would be like to be in a real touring group. Whoopee.

Someone knocked on the door. Sonny the roadie appeared. "Hey, guys, when you playing tonight?" he asked.
"Oh, not 'til about eight," Jed replied.
"Man, let's go down to Juarez!" he said, looking right at Jed. Of all of us, I guess Jed looked like the most willing candidate for the adventure.
"Garth, when are we setting up for the show?" Jed asked.
Garth was stretched out on the bed watching a football game, completely immobile, his mouth open and his eyes at half-mast. "We need to be over there by six-thirty," he answered in a monotone. "I don't care if you go, but you'd better be back in town by six." A slight pause. "*And* ready to play."
That left about four hours to go to Juarez, drink tequila, eat a worm, catch a disease, get knifed, sober up, and return to Las Cruces. Jed thought hard. He looked at Mike, then Tom, then me.
"Whaddaya think, boys? Wanna go to *Wharz*?" Jed by then could pronounce Juarez like a native.
"I don't know," Tom said. "That's cuttin' it pretty close."
I could tell Tom was considering the trip. Being the ex-flyboy, he'd seen a few Juarez-like sin dens on weekend furloughs. But Mike and I weren't crazy about the idea and we relayed our response to Jed with our eyes.
"Naw, I don't think so, Sonny," Jed said.
I thought Sonny would try to coax us further, but he didn't. "Well, then, can I hang out with you guys here?" Sonny asked.
"Sure," we said. Sonny must've been really bored to sit around with five sleepy guys from Oklahoma in a motel watching football on a perfect fall day. He was good entertainment for us, though. He spun a few yarns about Juarez,

109

telling us how he got stuck in jail one weekend without his parents ever finding out, and how he lost his virginity to some whore there when he was fourteen. Sonny's eyes were those of an old hobo: eyes that had seen so much that they were no longer capable of expressing surprise or pure joy. Eyes weathered far beyond their years. Eyes that lit up only when sharing anecdotes of decadence.

That night we played at the Student Union for the alums who had gathered for the weekend. This time we lived up to Buck's plaudit, and pretty well everyone danced during every song. After the gig the day before, we would have been happy just to hear the audience cough every once in a while. The crowd was a lot like the ones that came to Buck's Cimarron Ballroom: same general age group, same social strata, same love of two-stepping and waltzing. It was the connection Garth had been longing for since the moment we rode into New Mexico at dawn, that musical link between people all over the land. Seeing people get up and move to the music helped confirm his belief in the power of what he was doing with his life. There in Las Cruces—hundreds of miles from home and hundreds more from his dream in Nashville, there in New Mexico, Land of Enchantment, whence our band's name was chosen—is where I believe reality and fantasy began to merge in Garth's mind.

Immediately after the show, around 2:00 A.M., we loaded up the gear for the trek home. I, however, had made plans before the trip to fly back to Tulsa. It was midterm week, and I had an enormous amount of studying to do. I knew it would be pointless to try to study in Jed's truck on the way back, so I spent almost everything I earned that weekend for a quick ride back. It was worth it to me, but the other guys in the band, particularly Garth, weren't terribly happy that I was getting out of lugging the equipment and unloading it, not sharing in the band duties.

Since Las Cruces doesn't have a major airport, I had to take a thirty-minute bus trip to El Paso to catch my flight. Sonny gave me a ride to the bus station in the wee hours of the morning.

"Thanks for all your help, Sonny," I told him as I unloaded my travel bag.

"Sure, no problem," he said. "Next time you come back, we go down to Juarez."

"Yeah," I lied. "You bet. Looking forward to it."

Sonny drove off and I stood alone in a gravel parking lot in Las Cruces, praying that my bus had not already come by. After fifteen anxious minutes, the Greyhound pulled up and I boarded. It was too dark to see where the empty seats were. I felt around, stepped on a few feet, and finally piled into a seat next to an old man who reeked of whiskey. We drove south in the dark, the Greyhound's wheels lulling everyone to sleep except me. I stayed awake, clutching my travel bag and nudging the guy next to me every time he sagged into my personal space. After we arrived at the bus station in El Paso, I flagged a cab and told my Mexican driver to take me to the airport.

"We're about as close to Mexico as you can get, aren't we?" I asked, trying to make conversation. I actually tried to ask the question in the native tongue, seeing how much I could remember from my Spanish classes in high school. But when the driver started speaking at his normal clip, he sounded to me like someone reciting the alphabet underwater. I apologized and repeated the question in English.

111

"*Sí*. About ten blocks that way," he said, pointing south, of course.

"I've never been out of the country," I told him.

He turned his head back and looked at me. "What time your plane leave?" he asked. "I can take you there right now."

I knew his offer was more out of desire to get a bigger fare than true El Paso hospitality. I actually thought about it for a moment, but my good judgment quickly returned.

"No, thanks. I don't wanna miss my plane." But I was still curious about leaving the country for the first time, if only for a few minutes. My plane didn't leave for an hour, but it was not my nature to do something so risky. I decided I'd rather sit in an airport than get murdered in Mexico at three in the morning.

"By the way," I asked, "is that Juarez on the other side of town there?"

The cabbie let loose a long, wheezing laugh and then started coughing horribly. "*Sí*. You heard of Juarez, eh?"

"Sort of," I replied. At least I'd gotten closer to Juarez than the other guys.

I flew out of El Paso around 4:00 A.M., changed planes in Dallas, and arrived in Tulsa just as the sun was rising. I saw two sunrises that weekend. My mind and body didn't feel connected anymore. I was as mentally and physically tired as I'd ever been. So this is the romantic life of the touring musician, I thought.

As I landed at Tulsa International Airport, I imagined my bandmates to be somewhere near Amarillo, maybe at a roadside café, stuffing greasy hash browns and gallons of steaming coffee into their baggy, unshaven faces. I found out later that on the way back, the New Mexico Highway Patrol had pulled the caravan over and searched the vehicles for illegal immigrants. Fortunately, Sonny hadn't stowed away behind one of the speakers.

I went to my parents' house and slept the entire day, which blew the purpose of my spending $150 to get back home early to study. The rest of Santa Fe made it back to Stillwater around five that evening and dove into bed, completing the longest and most adventurous weekend in the band's brief history.

We had conquered New Mexico; next, the world. But first we had to play Bink's for the fiftieth time.

7

TRIALS, TROUBLES, TROYAL, AND TROY

The Thursday after our Las Cruces excursion, I was scrounging around in my kitchen for something to eat. In the cupboard were two boxes of Kraft macaroni and cheese, four cans of green beans, two cans of baked beans, and one dusty can of garbanzo beans that had been following me since I first moved to Stillwater in 1983. Even though college life for most students is blissful poverty, I was proud to say I was never so famished that I resorted to opening that can of garbanzos, but for some reason I never threw the thing away. As usual, mac and cheese looked to be the lesser of the evils that night, so I ripped open the box and began searching for a suitable complement. Usually it was tuna, which I would blend in with the noodles along with a box of frozen mixed vegetables, but one of my roommates had eaten the last can for lunch that day. So I looked in the refrigerator and found a plastic bag with a couple of weenies inside. They looked OK, but

I couldn't remember when I'd bought them or even if it was I who bought them. I went ahead and chopped them up, tossed them in the concoction, and choked the whole mess down. The weenies added an unusually salty flavor to this particular batch—not necessarily bad, but not necessarily good, either. Three-year-old garbanzo beans, I told myself, probably would have tasted a lot worse.

Around midnight, I awoke to the sound of my stomach churning and gurgling. For the next six hours, I systematically emptied every ounce of liquid and semi-solid from every orifice in my body. Never in my life was I even close to being that dismally sick. When I woke up in the early afternoon, I dragged my feeble, dehydrated body downstairs and made a call to Garth at DuPree Sports.

"Garth, this is Matt."

"Hey, man, howya doin'? Ready for tonight?"

"Well, Garth, actually I'm not. I'm sicker than hell."

"What's wrong? Gotta cold?"

"I wish. I'd rather have pneumonia than this." I proceeded to give him the gory details.

"Got ahold of some bad wieners, huh?" he laughed, still not convinced that I was all that sick.

"Garth," I said, "I don't think I can play tonight."

He stopped laughing. "Why not?"

"Well, I'm drained, man. Literally. I can't be more than ten feet away from a bathroom."

"Well, you'll be better tonight," he replied, trying to console me.

"If I'm not," I said, "do you think you can get someone to fill in for me?"

I figured that because it was just a Bink's gig, it wouldn't be any big deal. After a long, tense pause, he finally spoke.

"I can't do it, man. You're gonna have to play. I can't get anybody this late."

"What about that guy who filled in for me last summer?" Ron Beckel, a seasoned drummer from Oklahoma City who used to play with the Skinner Brothers Band, had filled in for me one weekend when I had to go to a wedding.

"Look, just plan on playing tonight. You'll feel better. We'll play shorter sets or something."

"But Garth—"

"I'll talk to you tonight. I've gotta go. Ed needs me out front."

I was completely taken off guard by Garth's unsympathetic response. I realized that when a substitute had to be found, which was rare despite one of us always being a bit under the weather, a chaotic gig was inevitable. Each song had to be explained to the sub, beginnings and endings got sloppy, and the whole rhythm of the show got lost in the shuffle. But I figured the rhythm would really be thrown off if I had to run to the john after each song, or during. After an hour of fretting and listening to my stomach wheeze like an old dog's, I called Garth back.

"Look, Garth, I really don't think I can do the show. I've never been so sick in my life. I can't even stand up for ten seconds without getting dizzy."

"How 'bout if we move your drums for you?" he offered.

"Garth—"

"I'll set 'em up myself."

"Garth—"

"I'll come by right after work."

"Garth—"

"O'Meilia, I need you to play tonight."

117

I couldn't believe the resistance I was getting.

"C'mon, Garth," I said, growing angry. "It's just a lousy Bink's gig."

To a man as devoted to performing as Garth is, that wasn't the thing he wanted to hear. After a long sigh, he finally mumbled that he'd try to get a replacement for me, that it wouldn't be easy, and he told me I was being a big weenie for copping out on him.

"*Please* don't say weenie," I said, then hung up. I didn't wait to hear if Garth found a replacement. I packed an overnight kit and immediately drove to my girlfriend Suzi's mother's house, located in a beautiful wooded neighborhood about nine miles west of Stillwater near Lake Carl Blackwell. It was my favorite place to go when I needed a break from the academic jungle, and just the secluded retreat I needed to hide from the band and recuperate. Normally I would have felt terribly guilty deserting friends in need, but I rationalized my escape by looking at the big picture: Would it matter in the grand scheme of things, as all huge rationalizations begin, if for one weekend Santa Fe gave a less-than-stellar performance? Everyone would still dance and get drunk. No one but the musicians would notice the little nuances that were missing, and they'd still get paid. It was just a lousy Bink's gig!

118

Fortunately, Garth located Ron Beckel and convinced him to drop everything and drive to Stillwater to take my place. The next morning I felt a little better, although I had not yet tried food, nor did I want to. I called Tom to ask about the show the night before.

"It turned out all right, I guess," he said. "Ron's a good drummer, but some of the songs were new to him."

"Is Garth still mad at me?" I asked.

"Well, he wasn't real happy about it. But if you're sick, you're sick, and there ain't nothin' you can do about it 'cept get better."

Finally some compassion. "Do you need me to play tonight?" I asked, praying he'd say no.

"Well, we told Ron he could play both nights since he had to haul ass over here from Oklahoma City. We'll get along all right without you."

The following two weeks, Garth and I didn't speak much. We never had a lot of in-depth conversations anyway, but we always clowned around, told bad jokes, and shared those special, seamy philosophies that males love to discuss. But all of a sudden there was a small iceberg between us. I half-expected him to fire me at any moment. My fears reached their zenith when he called a band meeting in the Bink's office before one of our Friday night shows.

"O'Meilia," Garth began, "I talked to the other fellas when you were gone a couple weeks ago." Jeez, here it comes, I thought: he's really going to fire me, and he wants everyone to watch.

"I told them to give Nashville some serious thought and then make a decision." I was relieved I wasn't getting canned, but now I had another heavy matter to think about.

"Well, uh, when do you want to go?" I asked.

"Pretty soon," he said. "As soon as we can, really."

I looked at the others. Each had chosen a different inanimate object to focus on while contemplating the move. Garth looked right at me.

"But I'm still in school."

119

"I realize that," he said. "Everybody here has something going on. Tom's got a wife and kid, Jed and Mike got jobs. I know Sandy's ready to do it. If you wanna go, we'll wait 'til you're done with school. What I need to know right now from you and everyone else here is who's going with me?"

Tom spoke up. "There's nothing I can do here that I couldn't do somewhere else. I mean, I can work at a post office anywhere. I think I'm ready to give it a try. Jeri's ready, too. She's been wanting to get out of here as much as I have."

"What about you, Michael?" Garth asked, acting as discussion coordinator.

"Well," he shyly began, turning slightly red, "I'm kind of inclined to go see what the Nashville *thang* is all about. Like Tom, I ain't plannin' on sortin' mail all my life."

120

Jed then volunteered his emphatic answer, "Hell, yeah, I'm going! I can't wait! There's nothing keeping me here. I'm a musician, man. I gotta try to make a good living at it while I'm still young enough."

It was my turn. After the Las Cruces trip and the horrible week afterward, I had begun to question the whole idea of living the life of a musical carny. Out loud I began to think the issue through.

"Um, I don't know. I mean, I really love playing in this band. I really do. You guys are excellent to play with and, uh . . . I've been in school for seven years now, and I—"

"Spit it out, O'Meilia," said Jed.

"Gimme a break, Jed, this isn't deciding what kind of ice cream I want. This is a major decision here."

"It's not that major if you know what you want," said Garth.

"Well, that's my problem: What do I want? I guess Nashville is the logical place to go to make a real living at this. But I've spent a lot of time getting this teaching certificate. Like you guys, I've wanted out of this town for a hell of a long time, too. But *Nashville?* I mean, this is a great band and everything, but . . ." My mind was flying so fast I was having trouble choosing the right words. Was I really getting ready to quit the band?

"Being a big-time country drummer just doesn't, you know, *mean* anything to me. The whole thing, country music, it doesn't mean anything to me."

The rest of the guys bowed their heads and tightened their lips. Garth, sitting chin in hand in the posture of a psychiatrist, didn't bat an eye. There was a long, terrible silence. I was ready and actually hoping for someone to try to persuade me not to leave, but no one said anything. I guess they expected it. Of all of us, I think I was the most surprised to hear those words come out of my mouth. It was a moment of self-understanding and supreme disappointment. Until that moment, I thought moving off to become a full-time musician was somehow in the cards for me. But even though I'd dreamed about it and talked about it from the first time I held two sticks in my hand, I knew deep down that when the time came to put up or shut up, my inexplicable, godawful fear of the unknown— the fear of both failure and success—would always force me to take the least dangerous path.

"OK, then," Garth said, seemingly unfazed by my decision. "I've got a few people in mind for a replacement. I want you guys to look around, too."

Just like that I was a lame duck. I agreed to keep playing until they found someone willing to make the big move.

121

Even though I was happy that I'd made such a big decision with some degree of confidence, I was very sad that I wouldn't be in the band anymore. Suddenly I felt like an outsider. As the others continued to discuss when they should move and where they should live, I just sat and listened, feeling extremely melancholy and suddenly thirsty for a cold one to drown the blues. I took some comfort in knowing that at last the path was cleared for me to wrap up my unbearably long academic career and move home the following spring, away from a town I had grown to despise for the same reason a marathon runner despises that last mile of the race.

"Hey, I know it's almost showtime," Garth said as the meeting finally drew to a close, "but there's one more thing. Randy Taylor 'n I wrote a song, a Christmas song, and we're going to record it out at Hufford's in a coupla weeks."

122

The next week we assembled at Tom's house to practice "Oklahoma Christmas." It was Garth's idea to record a Christmas song and try to get radio stations around the state to play it. It was a ballad about a big-time country music star living in Nashville who pauses to reflect on his simple days back in Oklahoma, pilin' into the ol' pickup truck with his brothers to go out and chop down a Christmas tree.

Mike Hufford had the only bona fide recording studio in town, with a sixteen-track mixing board, soundproof rooms, and the whole nine yards. Hufford—most people called him by his last name—is a burly, raspy-voiced, dark-haired jack-of-all-trades who back then wore big tortoiseshell glasses that magnified his perpetually squinting eyes. An experienced drummer, he sat in with about everyone who plucked or fiddled in Stillwater, including each of the members of Santa Fe at one time or another. And before Johnny Wright came along, Hufford was our sound man on certain occasions, including the Dwight Yoakam show and all the other big Bink's affairs. But recording was his bread and butter. He built his studio in the front yard of his property, comfortably situated in a rural area about five miles east of downtown Stillwater (five miles in any direction from Stillwater is rural). If you wanted to put together a demo tape or record some of your original songs, Hufford's was the place, provided you could scrape up the thirty dollars an hour or the twelve-pack, whichever Hufford was in the mood for, usually both. To put it mildly, things were not always serious business at Hufford Studios. Since it was a remote locale and you could get as loud as you wanted without disturbing anyone, Hufford's was routinely the place for local bands and their groupies to go after gigs for an impromptu, all-night jam session complete with an abundant supply of mood-enhancing goodies and lots of Hideaway pizza.

123

Garth had recorded with Hufford before and was well aware that our engineer might not maintain his keen musical perspective for the entire session. Hufford was one of the many Stillwater musicians I knew who had an incredible tolerance for spirits and such. Garth didn't mind all the beer and whatnot circulating around the studio as long as we got the cleanest recording possible. So other than stepping into the recording room to sing his bit, Garth stayed in the engineer's booth right alongside Hufford throughout the whole recording to make sure everything was done perfectly.

Garth invited our one-time potential bandmate, Dale

Pierce, to the session to play Dobro. Dale never got around to learning the steel guitar, so Garth never got around to bringing him on board, which was too bad because his banjo and Dobro expertise would have been a great addition to the group.

Garth, Tom, and I first laid down the rhythm track, with Garth singing a "dummy" vocal, one he could go back and sing over once all of the musical parts were complete. The biggest chunk of recording time involved Garth and the Skinner brothers getting their harmonies just right. After Jed made his contribution, Dale meandered into the recording room, adjusted the microphone and headphones, and started playing. When he began massaging that strange-looking instrument in his calm, stoic way, everyone in the engineer's booth suddenly stopped laughing and carrying on and just listened. Hufford, who always had a sly grin on his face, broke into an even wider smile as he twiddled knobs and moved levers up and down, his ever-present cigarette dangling from his lips. Santa Fe may have created the body of "Oklahoma Christmas," but Dale gave the song its heart, its lungs, and its blood.

"I think that's about got it," said our engineer, still functioning remarkably well in spite of all that he'd ingested.

"Wait a minute," said Garth, "I wanna try one more thing. You got any live crowd sounds?"

"I don't think so," said Hufford. "Why?" The rest of us looked at Garth, wondering the same thing.

"I wanna give this song a live effect," Garth explained, "like we're playing in front of twenty thousand people." Hufford scratched his head and then somehow remembered something.

"Wait a sec," he said. "I think we can fake it. I've done this before, I think."

Hufford began playing with some dials and brought up a loud hiss on the monitor. Then he did something to squeeze the hissing sound together, varying its volume and intensity, to sound like a live audience.

"Isn't this how Peter Frampton did 'Frampton Comes Alive?'" Jed asked.

"Yeah," Mike added, "we'd better be careful no one gets wind of this. Foolin' the public and all."

Garth laughed and finally loosened up a little. "Well, fellas, I'll tell ya," he said with a knowing grin. "It's all in the perception."

Hufford added crowd noise, with Garth's meticulous suggestions, to the beginning and end of the song. Then Garth went out into the studio and completed the "live" effect, adding to the beginning: 125

"This next song's one we did for all our friends and family back in Oklahoma. The number one state in the US of A!"

Hufford brought up the volume on the hiss/crowd as Garth said "US of A!"—making it sound as if we were playing at a political convention. As the song trailed off, Garth added to the illusion with:

"We love ya. God bless each and every one of ya. Merry Christmas."

After the tape was mixed, Garth sent it to radio stations around the state. He contacted the *Stillwater NewsPress* to do a story about the song. "We didn't get any money for the song," he said in the article. "We traded it to tell people to believe in Oklahoma, even during the bad times. We wanted to tell Oklahoma that we love this place and

Mike Hufford, 1995. Known as Hufford by his friends, Mike was Still-water's most prodigious recording engineer, thanks to his sophisticated studio and the festive recording environment he created. Photo by the author.

to hang in there." Garth was referring to the state's economy, which had been in a tailspin since oil prices began dropping in the mid-1980s. Because of the state-pride sentiment and the professional engineering of the song, major radio stations in Tulsa, Oklahoma City, and Enid agreed to play it, and "Oklahoma Christmas" made it to number eleven on the Oklahoma country charts. Billy Parker, a disc jockey from the Tulsa country radio station KVOO, was quoted in the same *NewsPress* article as saying our song was "very well accepted and very well requested." He went on to describe the sound of our band as "Americanish," whatever that means, and also said we were "just as good a band as ever came along."

We stayed very busy that winter, taking our Americanish sound to Enid's Bamboo Ballroom, back to Honky-Tonk Hell and Bink's, then on the road again to Norm's Country Ballroom in Ponca City, where I had an awkward meeting with the man who would assume my role as beat-keeper of Santa Fe, Troy Jones.

Troy was born in Wichita, Kansas, and he and his two brothers were reared by his father and grandmother in Blackwell, Oklahoma, a town of about ten thousand located seventeen miles west of Ponca City, just about an hour north of Stillwater. Growing up in Blackwell, you were in oil, zinc, or farming. When the zinc factory closed while Troy was in high school, two thousand people—one-sixth of the town—cleared out. But Troy's father was an oil man, so the Joneses stuck around, not knowing that a disastrous oil crunch would hit the town a decade later.

In the meantime, Troy did what most small-town high-school kids do: drink beer, smoke cigs, go to the lake, and listen to music with all of his friends who weren't forced out by the zinc bust. The Eagles were the first band to infect Troy's mind. Troy decided that to sing and play like Don Henley would be the ultimate musical goal. So he bought a set of drums from his uncle in 1974 and began

127

that wonderful journey toward annoying the hell out of the neighbors and everyone in his family. After a couple of years, he finally got up the courage to play with other musicians. He jammed in "barn bands," the country equivalent of garage bands. In Blackwell, there are a lot more barns than garages, so that's where they'd play. It was an awful racket, as you'd expect, so it was best that only cows and horses had to endure it. One particularly eventful night, Troy and a guitar player took their instruments and their shaky, adolescent voices out to a lake party and jammed. They passed a hat and, because everyone was drunk, people put money in it. Troy was in ecstasy. "This is it for the rest of my life," he said to himself. "Music is it."

From that lake gig, he and his guitarist were inspired to play as much as they could. Since they were still teenagers, they had to go out of town to play in bars because everyone in Blackwell knew they were underage. They ended up playing in nearby Cherokee and Alva, covering the Eagles, Creedence Clearwater Revival, Thin Lizzy, and Marshall Tucker. Just a guitarist and drummer. Imagine. But they played for six months that way, with the rinky-dinkiest sound system and no bass player, and actually got paid. After reaching the limit of what two poorly equipped teenagers could do, they finally found a bass player. But by then the guitarist had developed the unfortunate habit of drinking to excess and trying to beat up the entire audience. This led to a lot of near-muggings after gigs, so Troy decided to put music on hold for a while. And what better way to do so than to get married?

They were young (twenty), in love, and living in a small town. They tied the knot and shortly afterward had a daughter. Like his father, Troy got a job in the oil field to support his family. He came home every night dead-tired, soaked with sweat and petroleum. It wasn't the life he'd dreamed of, and his new bride wasn't crazy about it either. Like many another marriage that began with the seemingly boundless optimism of lovers just barely out of high school, the young Jones family ended in divorce after only a few years. Troy was divorced at an age before many people even think about getting married.

As the ensuing depression began to lift, he got the itch to play again. He heard about a rock band that was looking for a drummer. He auditioned but didn't make the cut. However, one of the guys in the band told him about some veteran local rockers who were interested in starting a country group. Troy made a call and suddenly found himself playing in one of Ponca City's most popular groups, the Kaw Dam Band. They played all of the local honky-tonks, including Norm's Country Ballroom, where they opened for Reba McEntire in 1984. They also made the band contest circuit, thinking that would be the sure ticket to stardom. After an appearance in the Marlboro Talent Roundup finals in Tulsa, when they played so well that they felt sure they'd won—but, alas, did not—the band quickly fell apart.

129

Like a moth to a flame, Troy again assuaged the musical hole in his life with female companionship, this time with a student at OSU. He moved to Stillwater in order to nurture the romance, and took a job with a construction company. One night in January 1986, he went out to throw back a few brews and ended up at Thumpers, a small club about two miles north of the Strip. There he saw Garth for the first time, over in a dark corner singing his guts out to no one in particular. But Troy paid attention. He'd never heard a bar singer belt it out like that. During a break, Troy went up and introduced himself.

"Man, you need a band behind that voice of yours," he told Garth. "You got one?"

"Nope," said Garth.

"Listen, I've got a tape of a band I was in up in Ponca City. You ever heard of the Kaw Dam Band?"

Garth shook his head. Troy invited Garth out to his car and plugged in the tape.

"Well, whaddaya think?" asked Troy, suddenly excited about getting the old band back together with this incredible singer he'd found.

"Pretty good sound," was all Garth could say. "Look, I've gotta get back inside for the next set. It was nice to meet you, man."

130   "Hey," Troy said before he left, "you let me know if you ever need a drummer."

"Thanks, Troy," Garth replied. "I might just do that."

A few months later, Garth started Santa Fe. Troy by then had started playing in a country trio called Nosmoking, playing around Ponca City and Arkansas City, Kansas. Four months later, Troy stopped by Bink's and saw us playing. He reintroduced himself to Garth during a break.

"Man, I knew you'd sound damn good with a band."

"Thanks, Troy," Garth said as he made the rounds with the Bink's crowd. "Nice seein' you again."

Troy didn't talk to Garth again for six months. Nosmoking got booked to play in Montana for a week, a kind of extended audition for a mini-tour of the state. The week before the Montana trip, Troy got word that I'd left the band and Garth was looking for a new drummer. A few months earlier, Troy would have left Nosmoking in less

than a heartbeat to play in Santa Fe. But things were looking up for his group. Plus, when you play in a trio you get
a bigger share of the pay. But he felt he should at least give
Garth a call. He did, and Garth told him the situation.

"Nashville, huh?" Troy said.

"That's what we're shootin' for," said Garth.

Troy told Garth his band was getting ready to drive to
Montana.

"Well, then," said Garth, "you'll have a lot of time to
think about it. So do."

We were playing at Norm's the night before Nosmoking hit the trail to Montana. Troy came in while we were
setting up. I was helping Johnny Wright tape down cords,
test microphones, and do other grunt work.

"Hey, man, I'm Troy Jones. You're Matt, right?"

"Yeah," I said, trying to place him as I shook his hand.
"How do I know you?"

"Oh, you don't. I've just seen you guys play a lot, know
who you are and everything. Where's Garth?"

"Backstage," I told him.

"I think that's one of the guys Garth's talking to about
replacing you," Johnny casually said after Troy left.

"Oh," I said like a robot.

Johnny sensed my melancholy. "Don't worry, you're not
out of the group yet."

"Yeah I am."

Troy found Garth in the back, and Garth introduced
him to Jed, Tom, and Mike.

"I can't stay long," Troy said. "I just wanted to come
over and watch a few songs. We gotta finish packing the
gear tonight."

"OK," said Garth. "We've gotta do sound check now.

131

Give me a call when you get back."

"I'll do it."

It was a cold, rainy night, and the crowd wasn't too big, so we were pretty loose onstage, pulling out songs we hadn't done in months and playing a lot of obscure requests. It turned out to be a throwaway night; we let our rock hair hang down and just went wild in one of the loudest Santa Fe performances ever. With Norm's at not even half-capacity, the sound was ricocheting all over the place. Johnny eventually threw up his hands, kicked back behind his sound board, and got drunk along with everyone else.

As soon as Troy got back from his Montana gig, he called Garth. A week later, Garth, Tom, and Jed drove up to Ponca City in a snowstorm to watch Nosmoking play a gig at a club called Chaps. They stayed for six or seven songs. Still not convinced Troy was the right man, Garth invited him to come audition with Santa Fe. Everyone knew about it but me. We were unloading the equipment at the Cimarron Ballroom when Garth walked in with Troy.

"Hey, O'Meilia," Garth said politely, "I got a favor to ask you."

"Sure," I said. When I saw Troy, it wasn't hard to figure out what he wanted.

"You think Troy here could, um . . ."

"Yeah, yeah, no sweat. Just let me get my drums set up."

"Could you hurry?" he added. "Troy's gotta play up in Ponca City tonight, and I've gotta drive him back and then make it back here for our show." I wondered why Troy didn't have his own car.

"OK, no sweat," I said, repeating a phrase the way people do when they get flustered.

132

"You want me to help you?" Troy asked.

"Naw," I said, "I can do it in five minutes. It's no sweat." As I bitched to myself and hurriedly set up my kit, it occurred to me that Troy was probably pretty nervous about the audition. I climbed off the stage and tossed him my drum key.

"You can arrange 'em however you like. But don't put a hole in the snare or I'll kill you." I meant it as a joke, but Troy was so nervous he thought I was serious. It was one of those uncomfortable exchanges when senses of humor are not in sync. "Uh, OK, I'll be careful," he said.

I sat with Johnny at the sound board and watched Troy and the boys play together for the first time. Troy's drumming was entirely different than mine. Much heavier. He pounded the high-hat like a blacksmith hammering a horseshoe. He was an arm drummer, whereas I was all wrist. I felt sorry for my poor drums with that wild animal thumping on them. But he was good and steady. After they had played a few songs, the others told Troy he had done a good job. He walked over and thanked me for the use of my drums. I said "no sweat" for the fourth time and, as Garth and Troy zoomed back to Ponca City, I went up onstage to see if Troy had broken anything. Jed came over to me while I rearranged my kit.

133

"Man, I thought it kind of sucked that you had to hurry and set up so Troy could audition."

"It's no big deal, Jed," I said, finally using a different expression to tell the same lie.

"Well," said Jed, "if I were you I would have told Garth to set the damn things up himself if he was in such a big hurry."

"I feel the same way," said Mike.

I knew they were trying to be nice and make me feel better about the whole situation. The way they were completely overreacting told me that. After all, it wasn't as if I was abdicating the throne or anything. I was just leaving a band that was going to go out to Nashville and disappear like ten million other bands. What did I care?

On the way back to Ponca City, Troy told Garth that Nosmoking had played so well in Montana that they had been asked to come back and play around the state from January through May. It would be easy money and some pretty decent perks, so Troy was seriously considering it, even though it meant five months in the dead of Montana winter.

"Well, I thought you played damn good with us," Garth told him. "But I gotta talk it over with the other guys first. You let me know if you decide you wanna go up to Montana and freeze your ass off." He dropped Troy off at his club and double-timed it back to the Cimarron.

As usual, Buck Dollarhide joined us that night, waltzing everyone into submission. Buck also brought up a couple of his other big, beefy buddies and commenced to get swing-happy, leading us through an entire set of Bob Wills numbers. It was like old times for everyone, including me: "Waitaminute, Buck. How's this one start?" But big, easygoing Buck didn't care if we got the beginnings or endings perfect, just that we got some of the stuff in the middle purty good. Buck seemed to be lost in a nostalgic haze that night, extending his stay onstage for at least half of the show. "Just one more," he said about twenty times. "Y'all know that 'Pig Sloppin' Blues?'" Maybe he'd had a few Scotches and started thinking about when he was a kid, figuring out songs on his three-string guitar as he

134

Trials, Troubles, Troyal, and Troy

sat in his bedroom with the Texas Playboys fighting their way through the static of his crummy little radio. It was his place, so he could do whatever he wanted. Everyone in the audience loved Buck, so they didn't mind stepping back in time with him. Sometimes it feels good to just remember what the music is all about.

8

I Can't Do This to Country Music

About the second week of December, Garth and the rest of the band decided to ask Troy to join Santa Fe. Troy said no at first, having promised Nosmoking he would go to Montana with them. But then he started thinking about that voice of Garth's, the voice that had mesmerized him when he first saw Garth crooning at Thumpers. That haunting voice eventually persuaded Troy to change his mind. We were setting up the stage at Bink's the night Garth told me Troy was going to take my place.

"Troy's got a few shows left with his group," Garth explained, "so he's not gonna, um, start playing until the last part of January."

Garth was uncharacteristically nervous, as if he were telling me someone had died. It was a relief finally to know when I'd be leaving. But almost the very moment I started the countdown to my departure, once the issue had been resolved and everything should have begun settling down, weird things began to happen. Depressing things. Things that eventually convinced me I had indeed made the right decision to quit the band. During my last month with the band, we seemed to be under a voodoo spell. Whatever it was, it was a bizarre transition phase for everyone in Santa Fe.

Strange Thing number one occurred that night at Bink's. Long before Santa Fe existed, there was a hot Stillwater band called the Barnstormers that regularly packed Willie's. In the band was one hell of a banjo picker named Buddy Watson. Buddy had dreams of making a living in music. He was happiest when he was in front of a crowd playing his beloved banjo, an instrument he'd become so attached to he actually gave it a name, Shelley, after the bluegrass song, "Shelley's Winter's Love."

138   On the evening of September 16, 1983, when Buddy was thirty-four, he was on the way back home from Tumbleweed when he got in a bad car wreck. Buddy was ejected from the car but not thrown clear; the car flipped twice and landed on top of him. He suffered a concussion but was still awake and alert enough to comprehend that his mangled left, chord-forming hand was trapped against the car's scalding catalytic converter. He was rushed to a hospital in Tulsa, where doctors told him the hand would have to be amputated. Buddy was in shock and unable to protest, but his brother, who somehow had heard about the accident and shown up at the hospital, told the doctors that Buddy was a banjo player, and begged them to try to save the hand. So the surgeons scavenged some tendons from Buddy's ankles and rebuilt the hand as best they could. The pinky finger, however, could not be saved.

For a long time Buddy could not accept that the accident really occurred. He couldn't even look at his banjo, so he placed it in its case and hid it in the closet. But after months of moping around, he decided that he loved the banjo too much to give it up for good. He took Shelley back into his arms and was surprised to find that, even though it was a struggle, he could form most chords. The sound of the ringing strings brought tears to his eyes. He decided that he would try to compensate for the loss of his pinky. Month after month he practiced, his tremendous heart urging him on despite a level of frustration that would have forced most people to give up. His efforts were rewarded, as the fingers of his left hand gradually became stronger and more dextrous than he thought possible.

Overcoming the physical obstacles to playing was difficult, but getting his mind in performance shape was even more of a challenge. Though he tried not to, every day he found himself staring off into space and reliving the worst day of his life: the sounds of glass smashing, metal compacting, his flesh sizzling, the sirens wailing, and the doctor telling him, "Buddy, I'm sorry, but there was nothing we could do about your finger."

Buddy and two of his friends walked into Bink's that night. Tom and Mike waved, knowing Buddy from their many years of hanging around Willie's. Buddy and his friends grabbed a table right by the dance floor and ordered a pitcher of beer. During our first intermission, Tom and Mike went over to talk to him. After they visited, Tom told me the tragic Buddy Watson tale.

"You know, I'd bet that even with four fingers he's just as good a player as anyone around," said Tom.

"Wow. He must've been hellacious at one time." I said.

"Oh, yeah. Ol' Buddy could get down."

139

By the end of our second set, Buddy had drunk enough courage to ask Tom if he could sit in with us for a song or two.

"I ain't played with nobody since the accident," Buddy warned, "but after sittin' here and watchin' you guys, I just gotta get up there again."

Tom was his usual gracious self and said yes, not really knowing what to expect. While Buddy went outside to get his banjo, Tom told Garth that Buddy wanted to sit in.

"Great," said Garth, who also knew Buddy from Willie's. "But can he, you know, still do it?"

"He says he's been practicing quite a bit. We're gonna find out right now."

Buddy reappeared, clutching Shelley and looking nervous. He was clad in a wrinkled blue denim shirt, blue jeans, and work boots. His blond hair and beard were unkempt, and his face glowed with a film of sweat. He was breathing hard. While Tom and Garth discussed what instrumentals we'd play, Mike began setting up a microphone for Buddy's banjo.

"That about where you want it, Buddy?" asked Mike. Buddy nodded quickly, saying nothing. He faced neither the audience nor the band, aiming his body at the left side of the stage where Tom's bass cabinet was. I usually made it a point to introduce myself to the people who jammed with us, but Buddy was staring at the floor, hunched over his banjo, so I left him alone. To satisfy my morbid curiosity, I tried to get a good look at his hand, but I couldn't. I think that's why he stood the way he did. Tom made an introduction:

"I'd like you all to welcome a good friend of ours who's gonna play a couple numbers with us: Buddy Watson."

140

Garth counted us off and we started together. The bluegrass beat magnetized several couples to the dance floor. Buddy bowed deeply over his instrument and started plucking. He was practically touching the neck of the banjo with his nose. The microphone on Buddy's banjo was turned up high in my monitor, so I heard it much louder than I could hear the other instruments. I knew the rhythm the rest of the band was playing, but Buddy seemed totally off in his own world. My first thought was that he was playing some kind of incredibly innovative jazz fusion banjo progression that was way over my head. I started shaking my head and looking at the other guys to see if I was the only one lost, but I couldn't get their attention because they too were all looking at Buddy and trying to figure out what he was doing. Soon we realized that Buddy simply had drunk just enough to upset his timing and rhythm.

141

Buddy suddenly stopped playing. He looked up from his banjo and stared at the puzzled, motionless people on the dance floor. He stumbled off the stage, made his way over to his table and collapsed onto it, sending his banjo and a full pitcher of beer crashing to the floor. Overcome by embarrassment and grief, Buddy began wailing loudly enough for the whole bar to hear. In a puddle of beer, his good hand covered his maimed one. The whole place just stopped. No one knew what to do. Finally a waitress went over to the table and began to mop up the beer. Buddy's friends helped him collect himself and the three quickly vanished.

I didn't want to play any more. Having just heard Buddy's story and then having his misery compounded before my eyes, I just wanted to go home and cry. But

Garth wheeled around and called for a peppy number to get everyone's mind off the horrible drama: George Strait's "Unwound," a song about a guy getting plastered to forget a girl.

That incident punctuated my career at Bink's. We probably played six months' worth of weekends there, and although some gigs were far more exciting than others, it was never boring. Bink and Mac Overholt always gave us something to talk about. We opened for old stars and new stars. We saw women dance naked. We saw fists fly and dreams die. We made a lot of people boogie and a lot of people go home and throw up. Bink's was where it all began. Bink and Mac sold the place about a year later and it became a secondhand furniture store. Now we can go back to Bink's only in our minds.

142

The next week we played our second four-night stand at the Ramada Inn lounge. The first time we played there was pretty uneventful. A hotel lounge is not a place to conquer. It's a place to be mellow, play softly, and stuff yourself during breaks on egg rolls and those little cubes of cheese on toothpicks. Tom informally dubbed us the Lounge Lizards whenever we played the Ramada. Jed liked the name so much he adjusted the lobby marquee accordingly. People who knew us and came to watch thought we'd really changed our name. The hotel guests who happened to wander downstairs didn't care who we were. To them, we were nothing but a diversion while they ate and had a martini before going back to their rooms to see what was on the free movie channel.

The lounge consisted of three long tables and a handful of round ones, arranged so closely together that you had to ask five people to move if you wanted to go to the bathroom. Completing the dim and oppressive ambience were sound-muffling carpet and ceiling, fuzzy wallpaper, neon beer signs, fake palm trees, and paintings of ships and fruit baskets and mountain scenes. The small buffet table by the lounge's entry was attended by a real French chef paying his dues in a place he'd never heard of until two days before he arrived. It was like playing in someone's overly decorated living room. The stage was a remote corner of the lounge. We didn't have a lot of equipment to begin with, but we had to scale down considerably when we played the Ramada, using the smallest amps we could find. Space was so tight that Jed and Tom had to sit on hard wooden bar stools to play, and Mike had to stand so close to me that I hit either his fiddle or his rib cage with my sticks at least once per song. After two nights of that, he'd had enough bludgeoning and wedged himself in between the front of my bass drum and Garth. But we'd played Willie's, so adjusting to cramped quarters was no big deal.

143

The last night the Lounge Lizards performed, on Saturday, the serpents awoke. The DuPree Sports throng filled up most of the place, and they let us know right off the bat that they weren't going to stand for us playing as if we'd been lobotomized. The manager didn't want us to get too loud, out of courtesy to the hotel guests. But it was our last show, so we joined in with the jovial and ever-inebriated Dupree gang and turned things up a few notches. Then weirdness began.

First, Mike threatened to pound my face in. After one song in which he had a solo, I made a lightheartedly sarcastic remark about his playing. Mike took it completely out of context and turned around to me with a face like

144   Group photo session after Troy Jones joined the band. (Troy is on the far left.) Gentle, easygoing Troy joined the band in January 1987 and provided the steady beat the band needed to energize its quest for stardom. Photo by Paul House.

a tomato, growling, "Well, why don't you come up here and show me how to play this fucking thing, you son-of-a-bitch." He was breathing hard and sweating. Maybe it was all the sticks I'd jabbed him with that week, or his inexplicable lack of confidence in the way he played, or the beer. Probably all three. Our bandmates were as confused as I was during this grotesque scene. I babbled something about how I didn't mean anything by what I'd said, apologizing like a maniac. We played one more song and then Garth decided it was time for a break. Mike apologized immediately after the set, saying he was on edge about something completely unrelated to me. I breathed a sigh of relief and headed off to the bathroom across the lobby. But I wasn't out of the woods yet.

As soon as I stepped out of the lounge, I saw my ex-girlfriend, Suzi. We had broken up about a month before, but it was a semigenial parting. She was standing with a large and very handsome guy whom she introduced as "a friend," which, of course, always means something more. I forced my best fake smile, exchanged pleasantries, then crossed the lobby to the bathroom with a big knot in my stomach. I walked in and saw two rough-looking types finishing their business. They were unshaven and looked as if they had just stopped in from a cross-country cattle drive. Both wore cowboy hats and dirt-stained dusters, those long cowboy trench coats. I assumed my position at the urinal, keeping a peripheral eye on the thugs. Suddenly the door swung open and in walked Raddler Shipley. He saw me, gave me a loud greeting—"O'Meilia!"—and took the stall next to me. The seedy-looking gents at the sink were annoyed by Raddler's salutation. One of them snarled, "Who's O'Meilia? What kind of stupid name is that?"

"He's the drummer, you asshole!" Raddler gently replied. Raddler's breath indicated he was feeling no pain.

"Well, he sounds like a pussy to me!" replied one of the bullies. He was right, of course, but that didn't stop Raddler's temper from flaring. Before he could respond, I whispered, "Cool it, Rad, I don't want to die." In the previous fifteen minutes, my heart and stomach had had enough anxiety to last me a year. Normally in such a situation, I would have given the guys five bucks to leave me alone. I am never straight enough or drunk enough to fight anyone. We weren't in any position to do anything about

145

their threats, anyway, as Raddler and I were still relieving ourselves. Raddler continued to trade barbs until one of the hard-asses announced, "We'll be waiting for you dicks out in the lobby."

After nearly a year of playing with Santa Fe and meeting real country fans, my fear of bloodthirsty rednecks had all but disappeared. Most country-bar goers were out to unwind a little, have a drink or two, dance, and possibly get laid. But suddenly one of my worst pre-country-band nightmares was coming true.

"Raddler, what are we gonna do?" I was shaking, and it wasn't from the draft down below. "I don't wanna fight anybody."

"I'll fight those pricks myself," said the brave, semi-conscious Raddler. "They can't talk about you like that."

"Rad, they could call me the most horrible thing in the world and I wouldn't care. They're just drunken idiots. Let's just get back to the bar."

We zipped up and walked out the door. Sure enough, the goons were standing in the lobby, egging us on. Raddler lipped off a little more while I made a beeline for the lounge. Raddler followed me in and started telling some of his DuPree Sports buddies about what had happened. One of them was a guy named Mark Cashen (name changed to protect the guilty). Mark was an extremely dashing, funny, mischievous fellow about twenty years old. He was the DuPree Sports clown, and also happened to be a football player and intramural boxer. After hearing what had gone down in the john, Mark smirked, put the collar up on his jacket in tough-guy fashion, and calmly walked out into the lobby with Raddler. I hate to see fights almost as much as I hate being in them, so I retreated to the drums and sat down. No one else was onstage yet, but I continued to sit. Garth came up and strapped on his guitar.

"You in a hurry or something?" he asked. I was usually the last guy onstage, so Garth knew something was up.

"Naw," I said, trying to be nonchalant, "there's just nowhere else to sit." The rest of the band soon joined us. Two songs into our last set, Mark and Raddler reappeared in the back of the lounge, laughing and slapping each other on the back. After the set, Raddler came up and gave me the grisly details.

"Ol' Mark walked out there and said, 'Which one of you called O'Meilia a pussy?' That one asshole said, 'I did, you son-of-a—' Then *splat*! Ol' Cashen nailed him." Raddler smacked his right fist into his left hand to dramatize the punch, making me wince. "There was blood on everyone within twenty feet. It was awesome! One punch and the guy was *gone*!"

147

"You've gotta be kiddin' me, Raddler," I gasped.

"No, man, you shoulda seen it. Then the guy got up and wanted more! His buddy finally dragged him out of there. I'm sure they went straight to the hospital." Raddler was beaming. He was so proud it made me sick. And it all started over some stupid name-calling. The next afternoon, I got a phone call.

"Is this O'Meilia?" the strange voice asked.

"Yeah. Who's this?"

"That was a cheap shot you got me with last night."

Gulp! My mouth instantly transformed into a tiny cotton field.

"Oh, no, man, that wasn't me."

"You know, I had to get my nose and jaw completely reset. It's gonna cost me a thousand bucks."

On and on went this nightmare conversation. Mark had apparently rearranged the guy's nose *and* jaw with one punch. And because it was my name that kept getting tossed around throughout the brawl, this guy, in the drunken haze of the night before, thought I was the one who had creamed him. Since I was the only one with that surname in Stillwater, it wasn't too difficult to find my phone number. *And* address. My supreme cowardice finally made me confess that I knew who had socked him but that I couldn't say his name. That was a mistake.

"C'mon," the voice demanded, "just tell me who it is and you'll be off the hook. Otherwise, I'm gonna think it was you."

"Man, I *swear* it wasn't me. If you saw me, you'd know in a second there's no way I could have hurt you. I'm built like Gandhi. Besides, anybody who hit you that hard would've broken his knuckles. There's not a scratch on mine."

"Well, I'll just come over and take a look," he hissed, "with a few of my buddies."

After he hung up, I put my fist to the side of my head and tried to figure out how one blow could disfigure someone so badly. My roommate, Sleepy, walked into the house, saw my blank stare, and asked what was going on. After I told him, he said, "Look, I've got a gun upstairs." That was all I needed to hear. I immediately went outside, jumped in my car, and floored it over to a friend's house to hide out. I came back later that night, expecting to see a bunch of dead bodies all over the lawn and Sleepy sitting on the porch blowing smoke out of a gun barrel. But the only thing that happened, thank goodness, was that the man without a face left several phone messages. I talked to him one final time the following week. He kept trying to make

Dale "Raddler" Shipley, 1995. In addition to being the group's main cheerleader and a confidant of Garth, Raddler defended certain band members from thugs. He also provided Santa Fe with its first practice hall: his backyard toolshed. Photo by the author.

me divulge the identity of his assailant. I simply lied as much as humanly possible, which is quite a bit when your life is at stake. Had I given him Mark's name, no one would have spoken to me again. By some miracle, the guy left me alone. But that potential catastrophe, along with the other incidents of bar-life mayhem I witnessed while in Santa Fe, made me more and more eager to put the band life behind me. Fortunately, I only had two more gigs.

My next-to-last show was on New Year's Eve. Garth booked us at the Bamboo Ballroom in Enid. For any band, playing on New Year's Eve means big money. It's the one night of the year when the value of musicians goes up, no matter how bad they are. Everyone's having parties and everyone wants a band, so musicians naturally exploit the demand and command outrageous fees. Garth milked the Bamboo management for a cool grand—two hundred bucks each. That was about three times what we normally made for a night. I guess the Bamboo folks figured the place would be packed on New Year's Eve so they could still make a huge profit. But sometimes the best-laid plans of mice and men go to hell in Enid, Oklahoma.

Enid, a city of about forty-five thousand, is in north-central Oklahoma, about an hour and fifteen minutes northwest of Stillwater. Even though it's a relatively short drive from point to point, the topography between the two towns is dramatically different. Stillwater is no more mountainous than Kansas, but compared to Enid it's like the Rockies. Ten miles outside Enid, the first thing that comes into view as you drive west on Highway 64 is one of the world's largest grain silos, constructed during the days when the town was known as the Wheat Capital of the World. It's truly an awesome edifice, particularly when contrasted against the miles and miles of flat, brown earth as far as the eye can see. A few miles further, you start looking at the people in your car and wondering who's got the sour stomach. Then you notice the gigantic sulfur plant on your left and realize why everything smells like rotten eggs. When you hit the first truck stop, you take a right onto an unmarked service road that winds into town. You pass over about fifty sets of train tracks, pass in front of the ominous-looking silo, make a sharp curve in front of the mental institution, then continue west about five miles until you see what looks like an enormous barn: the Bamboo Ballroom. But if you need to eat before you play, as we always did, you must first stop at what was then probably the world's only laundromat/restaurant, located about a mile east of the Bamboo. That's where we ate whenever

150

we played in Enid. I don't recall the name of the place, but whoever owned it made the best chicken sandwiches and chocolate milkshakes any of us ever had. Unfortunately, these were usually the highlight of our trips to Enid.

The Bamboo was certainly the oldest ballroom we ever played. It was built in the 1930s as an airplane hangar, then converted after World War II into the musical hot spot it is today. Elvis Presley supposedly played there once, although exactly how and why the King and his undulating pelvis wound up in Enid staggers the imagination. The whole place was made entirely of dark brown wood—no bamboo that we could see. The dance floor, like the town's surroundings, seemed to go on forever. It would probably take two hundred people to fill it. Some bands may have enjoyed that distinction, but Santa Fe didn't even come close. Our first performance there, we pulled in perhaps fifty people. On New Year's Eve, we may have doubled that.

The Bamboo was odd for several reasons. At most clubs or ballrooms we played, the owner or manager usually made it a point to come up and introduce himself to everyone in the band. But at the Bamboo, there was no charismatic soul like Buck Dollarhide or Mac Overholt sidling up to us to crack a joke or tell us a funny story about some terrible band that had played the week before. We just brought the equipment in through a door by the stage, set up, and started playing. To get a drink or go to the bathroom, we walked the half-acre to the back of the club. Otherwise, since we knew no one in Enid and few of our fans ever drove that far to watch us, there was no reason to wander too far from the stage. The Bamboo was a no-contact gig. Very few of the dancers even

151

came up to make requests, which was unusual. When the show was over, we packed up and escaped through the convenient side door, then waited in our cars while Garth went back to some smoke-filled office and collected the loot. Then we would hit the pitch-black road out of town feeling emotionally as flat as Enid.

I was home for the Christmas holidays, so I made the trek to Enid from Tulsa with three of my misfit chums, guys who were so far out of the social loop that on New Year's Eve, when any normal person can find a party by taking two giant steps in any direction, they actually wanted to drive to Enid and back—a four-and-a-half-hour trip—to watch my band play. I was glad they came with me, though, because the trip from Tulsa to Enid is probably the most nonscenic route in Oklahoma. Not only do you witness the desolation of Enid, but you also have to take the Cimarron Turnpike, the most bland stretch of road in the world—and you have to pay for it! Fortunately, most of the traveling was in the dark.

All pretty happy to be making so much money for one show, we were loose and relaxed. After the stifling Ramada gig two weeks before, it was great to be able to spread out again, especially for Garth and Jed. Garth did his damnedest to get the sparse audience out of their booths and onto the floor. As he always did, during the first set he made a mental survey of the general age group of the patrons, what they wore, what kind of mood they were in, and then called out songs accordingly. After our first few months of playing, we stopped using song lists. Garth was a human song list. His memory amazed us all. He could instantly bring to mind not only any song we regularly played but also the obscure ones we did on occasion. I don't know how he did it, much less how he remembered those thousands of song lyrics. He never used cheat sheets or anything. Garth must have determined this particular crowd to be a bunch of 1950s throwbacks because we did a lot of old rockers that night, some Ventures instrumentals like "Walk, Don't Run" and "Wipeout," and a bunch of classic Everly Brothers, Buddy Holly, and Chuck Berry tunes. Garth and Jed were duckwalking all night. Even if the Bamboo management didn't make a profit that night, Garth made sure they got more than their money's worth.

It was a cold, cold early morning when we broke down the equipment and piled it into Jed's truck. The wind was whipping across the barren landscape, attacking everything in its path. To warm up and wake up, we each grabbed a big cup of joe from the Bamboo bar. We scraped the frost off the windshields, hopped into the vehicles, and cranked the heat while waiting for Garth to return with our biggest payment ever. He finally came over to my car and I rolled down the window.

"Nice job tonight, O'Meilia," he said, sniffling as he handed me an envelope stuffed with wrinkled tens and twenties. He honked into his handkerchief.

"You gettin' a cold?" I asked.

"I think so," he said. "I feel like crap."

"Well, we don't have to play next week, so you'll be all right for the City Limits gig."

"I sure as hell hope so."

"Hey, Garth," I said, extending my gloved hand out of the window, "Happy nineteen eighty-seven."

"Yeah, you too, man."

He hopped into his Jimmy and we caravaned out of Enid, past the sulfur plant and into the windy, wide-open

153

Oklahoma plains. When we hit I-35, Garth and company turned south and my companions and I continued east to Tulsa. I dropped them off and finally climbed into bed about 5:00 A.M.

The following weekend, I loaded my clothes and necessities and drove back to Stillwater for my final semester of college. Many times I'd told myself I was going back for only one more semester, but something had always happened to prevent it from being the last. This time it was set in stone: I would go to school until the middle of March, then move back to Tulsa for a half-semester of student-teaching at a local high school. After that, Stillwater would be forever a memory. And soon, so would the band.

154

For years, Tulsa was the site of the International Finals Rodeo, the biggest rodeo there is. So it was a very big deal to Garth that we were booked the week of the IFR at the Tulsa City Limits. The Tulsa City Limits management was promoting the club at the Tulsa Fairgrounds, where the IFR was being held. With a potential audience of people from all over the world, Garth was pumped up to do the ultimate show. Unfortunately, the hex that had begun the night Buddy Watson broke our hearts was not yet over.

We were scheduled to play four nights, Wednesday through Saturday. I was glad we had four shows because it was my last gig with the band and I needed all the money I could get to last me through the semester. We were loading the equipment at Tom's house on Wednesday afternoon when Garth showed up.

Mike, Tom, Jed, and Garth. This photo was taken for a *Stillwater News-Press* article that discussed the band's January 1987 Tulsa City Limits shows. Photo credit: *Stillwater NewsPress.*

"What's going on, boys?" he said. Garth sounded as though he had a sock in his throat.

"What's the deal with your voice?" asked Jed.

"I don't know, man," he wheezed. "I can't shake this crap, whatever it is."

"Are you gonna be able to sing?" asked Tom.

"I think so."

"Well, if you can't," I offered, "then maybe Tom and Mike can do the vocals."

Garth acted as if he hadn't heard me. He popped a throat lozenge in his mouth and announced with determination: "I'll be able to sing."

We loaded the gear and took off down Highway 51 to Tulsa. All the way, Garth said nothing, trying to preserve his voice as much as possible. We arrived at Tulsa City

Limits and got the stage set. Garth had Jed do all the mike checks, still afraid to strain his voice. Garth was used to occasional sinus problems; several times in the past he had had to sing with a less-than-perfect voice. When this happened, he'd usually call for a lot of Merle Haggard, George Jones, and Randy Travis craggy-voiced songs to mask his throat problem. But this was probably the biggest gig we'd ever had. Garth was noticeably concerned, almost angry about the condition of his voice. He told us that as soon as the show began and he got through a few songs, he'd be OK. We had no reason to think otherwise; he was the most consistently hale member of the group.

We eased into the set with "Diggin' Up Bones," a low-key tune with a lot of backup vocals by Tom and Mike. No problem. Then we picked it up a little with the Nitty Gritty Dirt Band's "Partners, Brothers and Friends." Midway through the song, it became obvious that Garth was straining. We finished the song and Garth quickly turned things over to Tom for two numbers. Tom usually sang lead on about fifteen of the tunes in our repertoire, but having fronted bands for many years, he could have sung for an entire show if necessary.

After Tom did Steve Earle's "Hillbilly Highway" and Bruce Springsteen's "Cadillac Ranch," Garth took over again and we played "Amarillo by Morning." Garth finished the song, but during the last couple of stanzas, no one could hear him. With each verse his voice was gradually disappearing. At this point, I expected Garth to turn over the reins to Tom and Mike, with Garth singing backup whenever he could. Mike didn't sing lead on any songs, although he probably could have if he hadn't been so doubtful about his talents. But playing at the Tulsa City

Limits in front of a big crowd wasn't the place for him to try singing lead. The band had reached a point many months before where my singing had become both un-necessary and detrimental, or I would have offered to sing the songs I knew, And Jed, as good a guitarist as he was, couldn't sing in key to save his life. Garth walked to the microphone, cleared his throat as much as he could, and made an announcement:

"I'm sorry, ladies and gentlemen. We're not going to be able to continue tonight. I hope you all come back to-morrow night and the two nights after that, 'cause we're gonna get everything straightened out and help you all have a real good time. Thanks and God bless all of you. Good night."

We walked offstage and the Tulsa City Limits DJ scram-bled to his booth to spin records the rest of the night. We went straight to our cars and drove back to Stillwater. It was depressing. Garth was obviously the most upset of all, but seemed sure he'd be able to play the next night. "I'm going to my doctor tomorrow to get this taken care of," he whispered.

The next night, Garth seemed like a new man. I don't know what his doctor gave him, if anything, or if he ac-tually went to the doctor at all. He told us he had taken the day off from work to relax. He was still hoarse, but he said he had sung at home a little without any problem. So once again Santa Fe took the stage to demonstrate to the representatives of the world's cowboys and cowgirls that Oklahoma had one hellacious band.

Garth sang the first song fairly well, but during the sec-ond, with his voice fading out with each word, he turned around and told us to stop playing. He approached the microphone slowly, bowed his head and sighed. "Folks," he began, too ashamed to lift his eyes from the stage floor, "I can't do this to country music." He was nearly in tears. "I'm sorry about this, but my voice is gone. I hope you all can forgive us."

I can't do this to country music. It was an odd thing to say, even for melodramatic Garth. It was as if Garth felt he were somehow jeopardizing the integrity of country music. But he had his reasons for saying it. He also had his reasons for not wanting the Skinner brothers to take over the singing chores, although no one knew what those reasons were. As we started to walk off, the crowd began clapping, the kind of applause given when injured football players are carried off the field. I glanced out into the audience and saw Craig Skinner, which gave me an idea.

158 "Tom," I said, out of Garth's earshot, "why don't we get Craig up here to do an evening of Skinner Brothers stuff?" It made perfect sense to me. The Skinners knew a million songs. Then Garth could rest his voice and perhaps sing the following night.

"I don't think so," he said.

"Why not?" I asked, confused.

"I don't think the Tulsa City Limits wants to hear us. They paid for Santa Fe."

"But the audience would rather hear a band than than the damned stereo system, wouldn't they?"

"Yeah, I guess," said Tom. "But I don't think Garth would be very happy about it." Jed overheard what we were talking about and agreed that we should try to finish the night with the Skinners. More than anything, I wanted to play because it was my last gig with these guys. I wanted to go out with a bang, four nights of country-rock chaos.

My other reason, running a close second, was the money. The less we played, the less we made. Then Garth came back to the dressing room with some bad news. "The manager said we should go ahead and pack it up," he rasped with what little voice he had left. "We're done." He had the longest face. "I'm sorry, guys."

I couldn't believe my country days had ended so abruptly. I went over to Garth and asked him what he thought about doing a Skinner Brothers set.

"Too late," he said. "They already told us to clear the stage. They said they'd get another band for the weekend."

"Jeez, Garth, this is my last gig."

"I know, man. No one wanted to play tonight worse than me. I'm sorry I let everyone down."

"You didn't let anyone down," I said. "If you're sick, you're sick. There's nothing anyone can do about it."

We tore down the stage while the Tulsa City Limits crowd practiced the latest line dance. I helped load the equipment for the last time. I ended up in the Skinners' parents' big Ford LTD with all three brothers. Garth drove back to Sandy's parents' house in Owasso to nurse his sore throat and depressed mind, and Jed and Johnny Wright rode in the truck. We stopped at a Quik Trip in Tulsa to gas up before hitting the road. Tom started the pump, then he and Craig went into the store to get a Coke while Mike and I sat in the car. All of a sudden we heard loud voices. We looked out of the window to see two guys arguing at the pump next to ours. Within seconds they started punching each other, and the fistfight quickly turned into a wrestling match. The two grapplers then started rolling around on the hood of our car. Before Mike or I could react, out of the Quik Trip bolted six-feet-two, 260-pound Craig Skinner. Like an enraged bull he ran over and picked up each of the gladiators and tossed them like two kittens.

"You boys take your fight anywhere but on my parents' car," Craig yelled, pointing his trembling, meaty finger in their faces. They got up and ran like two frightened schoolkids.

"Good God, I'd hate for Craig to be pissed at me," I said to Mike.

Mike sighed. "It's not one of life's more pleasant experiences, I can tell you that."

Tom came out of the store and he and Craig checked the hood for damage. Seeing none, they climbed into the car and we drove back to Tom's house in Stillwater to unload the equipment. After I packed the drums in my car, I went back inside. Everyone had sat down in the living room to watch TV and have a beer. I didn't feel like hanging around.

"Well, guys, I enjoyed it," I said, trying to say goodbye without appearing too choked up about it. "This was the best band I was ever in."

"So why in the hell are you quitting?" asked Johnny, the man who never cut anyone any slack.

"Yeah, man," continued Jed, "you think we're just a bunch of hicks? Do we smell bad? What the hell you want to be a teacher for?"

"So I can keep people from growing up like you, Jed." It hit me then that even though I would never have fond memories of setting up and tearing down equipment every weekend, I would miss being around the guys in Santa Fe. Had I not desperately needed money at one time, I probably never would have met them. I felt a curious mixture

160

of melancholy and relief.

"I guess I'm gonna head home," I said, not wanting to prolong my departure any more than necessary. "It's been an experience."

"Take it easy, Matt," said Tom. "Maybe we'll play again sometime."

"Yeah, maybe. Anyway, good luck to you guys. Hope everything works out all right."

"See you later, traitor," said a smiling Jed.

"Thanks for those warm words, Jed. And thanks for making me deaf with that chain saw of yours."

"My pleasure."

"By the way, tell your new drummer he can find a wide selection of ear plugs at any hardware store."

I had planned to stay in Tulsa the weekend of our Tulsa City Limits gig. But since our show had been canceled, I stayed in Stillwater, with no band, no girlfriend, no money, and absolutely nothing to do for the first time in nearly a year. My roommate Sleepy and I drank beer and listened to his scratchy old Doc Watson and John Prine albums. We sat on the porch and smoked pipes and played Frisbee in the front yard. It was great being just a college student again—free from playing those loud, violent bars and coming home at 3:00 A.M. stinking of sweat and smoke, with my ears ringing so much that I couldn't think straight, and with my mind a surreal mural of the faces of all those crazy, drunken, dancing, honky-tonk–addicted fools, until sleep graciously came to wash it all away.

161

9

End of the Road

Troy got his first workout with Santa Fe at the Ramada Inn lounge, site of the bloodbath a month and a half earlier. It was the band's first gig since Garth's voice deserted him at Tulsa City Limits. But Garth was back on form, and this time there were no loudmouthed hoodlums or fiddler flare-ups to spoil the party; only the peaceful, easy mellowness that goes hand in hand with serenading the hotel set.

Because of Troy's more conventional style and previous country-band experience, it didn't take him long to get into the swing of things. By the end of the four-night stint at the Ramada, he was comfortable with the band and vice versa. But performing for ambivalent, travel-weary audiences was no longer comfortable for Santa Fe, so Garth asked the Ramada management if they could begin playing weekend-only gigs there. They refused, and when Garth persisted, Santa Fe was abruptly fired from future Ramada service. Never was a band more relieved to get the axe.

The band began to put a percentage of earnings in a Nashville fund, intended to supplement living and traveling expenses, equipment purchases and, if necessary, rations. But while they continued to talk about Nashville, dream about making it big, and plan the physical move, Tom feared that they weren't making sufficient musical preparations. Santa Fe was good, but countless good bands had moved to Nashville only to be eaten alive. Tom had played in a lot of bands and knew the feeling of performers playing as one, that intangible energy which separated the good bands from the great. He knew Santa Fe had the potential to be great but wasn't quite there. Many times he suggested to Garth that spending more time on original songs would help develop that magic. But Garth seemed to think they already had the magic, and that nonstop performing would make it even better.

164

So Garth lined up weekend after weekend at the usual places. They played Willie's, slept through a few at the Bamboo, did Bink's when absolutely necessary, and waltzed several weekends away at the Cimarron Ballroom. They hit a few new places, too, playing an OSU veterinary medicine faculty party, Graham Central Station in Oklahoma City, the Bristow Elks Lodge, and the Lazy E Arena in Guthrie, Oklahoma.

In April, a little more than a year after stumbling through its first gig at Bink's, Santa Fe began its Nashville-or-Bust tour, performing at favorite spots for the last time. At the final Willie's show, banners were strung around the bar saying, "Good Luck, Garth. Stillwater Is Going to Miss You." It was déjà vu city for Garth. Only two years before he had stood there alone, leading everyone

Garth at Tulsa City Limits, 1987. This was Santa Fe's last TCL gig before moving to Nashville. Garth was determined to make the performance memorable in a positive way, unlike the previous show when his voice gave out and the band had to cancel its engagement. Photo by Jana Shipley.

in "American Pie" and thinking he'd never see the place again. Now he was back with a band, *his* band, and as he led Santa Fe through an emotional evening full of teary-eyed tributes to the Willie's crowd and the management, he knew that if he didn't make it in Nashville this time, there was no way in heaven, hell, or earth he'd come crawling back to Willie's to pick up the pieces. Even if he only got a job swabbing the floors at the Grand Ole Opry, he was going to become part of Nashville.

And the band played on, making final stops at the Cimarron Ballroom and Bink's to equally well-wishing crowds. After leaving Santa Fe, I made every effort to avoid seeing them play, even when they were performing on the Strip, which was only two blocks from my house. Although Troy was one of the humblest and most likeable guys I'd ever met, I didn't care to watch someone else play drums with Santa Fe. It would have been like bumping into an ex-wife and her new husband. Besides, I was too busy with my own farewell tour as a college student, studying a little and drinking a lot at the Stonewall Tavern with Sleepy and some of my other academically exhausted friends.

After I moved back to Tulsa to begin my student-teaching assignment, I heard Santa Fe was coming to Tulsa City Limits for its last show there. The anxiety I had about watching my old band gave way to curiosity to see how they sounded. It was Ladies' Night, meaning that all the females who arrived before ten got to drink free. So there were plenty of loose cowgirls when I showed up; not that it made any difference to a wallflower like me. I slipped up to the nearly empty balcony section and took a place behind the sound board. Some guy from Marlboro was walking around passing out free cigs, so I grabbed a few packs and pretended I was just one of the crowd. Santa Fe was in the middle of its second set when I sat down. They sounded cleaner and more professional than I'd expected. Down below I saw a big group from DuPree Sports, including Raddler and Mark Cashen, the face mangler. When the set was over, I went downstairs, climbed the stage's unlit and extremely perilous steps, and walked into the dressing room like I owned the place.

"Hey, boys, y'all sound great," I announced. How'd y'all like a big fat record deal right here and now?"

I expected to be greeted like the prodigal son but nobody even noticed I'd come in. The dressing room was packed with about twenty people, all smoking and drinking and carrying on. Everyone was engrossed in conversation. I met eyes with Tom and Mike, who acknowledged me with a smile and a raise of the eyebrow. Jed and Troy were sitting on the couch with two women and didn't look as if they wanted to be disturbed. Garth was shooting the bull with a man I didn't know. I felt as though I'd barged into a stranger's house.

167

"Come to beg for your job back?" Jed yelled at me from across the room.

"You're all heart, Jed," I replied. Then my brain froze. I couldn't think of anything else to say, and I began to wonder why I'd gone backstage. I hadn't spoken to any of them for about four months. It was foolish to assume I could have the same rapport. I weaved my way over to Troy, who offered me no challenge in reestablishing a connection because we'd never had one.

"You sound great, Troy. How're you likin' it so far?"

"It's awesome, man," he gushed. "It's finally startin' to come together. You know we're moving to Nashville next month?"

"Next month, eh? Well, that's, uh, awesome."

I couldn't fully grasp the idea that they were really moving to Nashville, the incredible uncertainty of packing all your stuff and transporting it to a strange city hundreds of miles away to play music and hope to make any kind of decent living, much less get famous. Especially Tom and Jeri, with young Jeremy to care for. I envied their optimism and bravery.

Before I left backstage, I briefly chitchatted with Tom and Mike. Garth was still busy talking to the same person, so I just waved at him and he gave me a little nod while continuing to talk. I was going to tell him the band sounded great, but I figured it wouldn't matter one way or another. I left the dressing room and walked over to the DuPree's gang.

168

"How's your student-teaching going?" Raddler asked.

"OK, I guess," I said. "The kids don't do anything I ask 'em to do, so I suppose I'm learning what teaching's really like."

Just then Santa Fe walked onstage and started their set. While they were playing, Raddler leaned over and yelled in my ear, "Do you miss playing in the band?"

"Naw," I said. "I wish I did, but I don't."

My curiosity thoroughly satisfied, I got up midway through the third set and said goodbye to the DuPree's folks, then waved to my former bandmates, who couldn't see me with the stage lights blazing in their eyes. I walked toward the exit feeling like a ghost among the living, a profound malaise creeping over me. As I stopped to take one final look at the guys onstage, it hit me that I had come to a place where nothing appealed to me: drinking, getting

Santa Fe at their last Tulsa City Limits show, April 1987. Johnny Wright is on the far right. Photo by Jana Shipley.

rowdy, dancing, playing cowboy music, playing music at all. Absolutely none of it gave me any enjoyment anymore. I wondered where my passion had gone, and if I truly ever had any.

Norm's Country Ballroom in Ponca City was chosen as the site for Santa Fe's last show in Oklahoma, in May 1987. Just before showtime, owner Norm Brown seized the moment and gave a generous and incredibly prophetic introduction.

"Folks, I'm glad you're here 'cause this is gonna be a real special night. After tonight, these boys here are headin' out to Nashville and, let me tell you right here and now, they're gonna be the biggest damn thing country music has seen in a long time."

The crowd whooped and hollered. An ex–Las Vegas drummer, Norm exercised his natural flair for commanding the attention of an audience. Like Buck Dollarhide, he was always looking for an opportunity to jump onstage to share the spotlight with the bands who played his club.

"So you'd best shine up yer shit-kickers and pack this dance floor, 'cause it's gonna be the last time you'll see a band this good in a li'l ol' honky-tonk like this."

The crowd yahooed and yeehawed. Norm turned to face Garth, who along with the rest of the band was wondering when the introduction was going to end.

"And I'll tell you another thing. What you're about to see is the real McCoy. I've watched Garth do his thing for a long time now, and I'd bet my last nickel that he's gonna be bigger 'n anyone." Norm picked up steam as the Garth face reddened and beamed. "So folks, let's give a big fat Norm's Country welcome to the next monsters of country music: Garth Brooks and Santa Fe."

A one anna two anna buckle my shoe . . .

———————————

"Hi, Stephanie, this is Bob Childers. Look, there's a guy from Stillwater who sings and writes coming out here in a couple weeks. His name is Garth Brooks."

"Is he good?"

"I can't remember. We played one songwriter night together at a club back in Stillwater, but I don't know him, really. Know his band real well, though. Jed Lindsey and the Skinners wouldn't be backing a guy who sucked."

"You think he's serious?"

"I can't be sure. I can try to size him up when he gets here. I know he's been here before, a couple years back. Lasted about a day, Jed said. So at least he's got the guts to try it again. Jed seems to think the guy's pretty focused now."

"You can lose your focus pretty quick here."

"Tell me about it. Anyway, he and Jed are going to stay with me while they look for a place for their whole band to live. I thought you could talk to him a little, maybe introduce him to that friend of yours."

"You mean Bob Doyle?"

"Yeah. The ASCAP guy."

"Maybe. I'll have to see. Let me know when he hits town."

171

Bob Childers was a Stillwater songwriter who moved to Nashville in the spring of 1986, just after Santa Fe was formed. He settled in the heart of the city, in a section called Third Coast, near Music Row. He was forty-one and a very recent divorcé. His two young boys were back in Oklahoma with their mother, and their absence in his life was nearly unbearable for him. To add to his woes, he was also recently made jobless, having been forced to quit his apartment-managing position after a bizarre mishap in which a screwdriver went through his eye. He was trying to decide if he should be in Nashville at all when Jed called to ask whether he and Garth could temporarily lodge at his modest two-bedroom apartment. Thinking their visit might take his mind off of everything else, he agreed. He also thought he might be able to feed off their excitement and renew his own purpose for being in Nashville. Besides, it couldn't hurt to meet another aspiring singer. It was in the interest of all Nashville songwriters to know singers—serious singers—and promote them any way they could. Only the seriously dedicated singers, though, were worth knowing because only they understood that it took anything and everything to land a record contract. And if a songwriter helps a singer get a record deal, then often the favor is returned: the singer chooses his helpful songwriting friend's songs to record. A year of playing writer's nights and showcases in Nashville taught Bob a lot about the Nashville back-scratching system. It also introduced him to a lot of fellow songsmiths, including a wily woman from Florence, Alabama, named Stephanie Brown, who had been in the songwriting game a year longer than Bob. The night Garth and Jed arrived in Nashville, Bob told Garth about Stephanie.

"I gotta meet her, man," said Garth, not feeling the least bit tired after the twelve-hour drive from Stillwater, fueled by a combination of excitement and apprehension at being back in the city of his dreams.

"Well, I've already told her about you, what little I know," said Bob.

"What about tomorrow? Can I meet her tomorrow?"

"I don't know. I'll have to ask her."

"Aren't we going to look for a house tomorrow?" asked Jed.

"Oh yeah. Well, there'll be time for that. Bob, can I use your phone?"

"Sure. It's right there in the kitchen."

"Uh, you got one back in the bedroom? I need to talk

to someone kinda private. And Sandy."

"Make yourself at home, Garth."

After Garth disappeared, Bob and Jed got reacquainted in the living room.

"So, is he serious about this whole thing?" Bob asked, pointed to the closed bedroom door. Behind it the two could hear Garth's muffled voice and frequent laughs.

"Yeah, I'd say so," said Jed. "Too serious, actually."

Fifteen minutes later, Garth came out of the bedroom.

"I'll be right back. I've gotta go see somebody."

"Where you going, man?" asked Jed. "Got a date?"

"Sort of," said Garth. "I've just gotta go meet someone. I told him I'd look him up when I got to town."

"Who is he?"

"It's nobody. By the way, Bob, do they sell Moon Pies in this town?"

"Moon Pies? I don't eat 'em so I don't know."

"Well, we stopped at a gas station after we got into town and they didn't have any, so I'm prayin' they've got some around here somewhere. If not, Sandy's gonna have to send me some."

"Hey, I've let a lot of weirdos stay here before, but I've gotta draw the line on Moon Pie addicts," said Bob.

"You guys got cigarettes and beer, I got Moon Pies and Coke," Garth laughed. "The more artificial ingredients, the better." Garth vanished into the night.

"Who does he know in Nashville?" Bob asked Jed.

"Hell if I know."

When Garth returned that night, Bob was still up, but Jed had passed out in the spare bedroom, exhausted from the long day's trek and the strain of lifting about ten beers to his mouth. Garth and Bob sat down together in the living room. Bob knew it wasn't his business to ask where Garth had been, so he didn't.

"Bob, I left here in kind of a hurry, so I didn't get a chance to thank you for letting us crash here while we look for a house."

"Hey, no problem. Stillwater guys gotta stick together. Know what I mean?"

"Yeah, I do. I know exactly what you mean. But I'm going to pay you for however long we stay here. And for any long-distance calls I make."

"Don't worry about it. I don't need it that bad," Bob lied. "You guys'll need all your money to stay alive out here."

Garth looked around at the small, shabby apartment. "It's OK. The band's got money budgeted for this. I'll pay you." He leaned forward in his chair and looked Bob squarely in the eyes. "To be real honest, we gotta be careful about who we're gonna owe favors to in this town."

Bob smiled. "I respect that. Speaking of favors, I talked to Stephanie after you left. She wants to meet you and Jed tomorrow night."

"Wow, I can't believe it."

"You got a demo tape?"

"Of course. It's not great. Some originals we recorded out at Hufford's. Remember Hufford?"

"Like my first kiss. How's he doing?"

"Hangin' in there. Still nuts."

"Garth, you want to know the first thing Stephanie asked me when I told her about you coming out here?"

" 'Is he fat?' "

"Almost. She said, 'Is he *serious*?' "

Garth sighed and leaned back in his chair. For a moment he stared off into space and looked as if he were about to

174

cry. The sudden long silence made Bob feel uneasy. Finally Garth stood up and began pacing around the room.

"Ever since I ran away from this place I've been trying to get back. I was such a dick, thinking Nashville needed me. Now I know it's the other way around. I need Nashville. I need to sing and play music for a living. There is simply nothing in this whole world I want more. Not sex, not food, not money . . ."

"Not Moon Pies."

". . . not Moon Pies, not air, not water. Playing and writing and singing music satisfies me more than all of that stuff put together. Music *is* sex and food and water to me. I don't know why, it just *is*."

"You realize that a lot of guys are passionate and determined and still never make it," interjected Bob, the cold voice of reality.

175

"I know that, but I can't worry about them. I can't worry about the odds being stacked against me. People come to this town with big dreams, but deep down they're expecting the worst. They're waiting for the system to bite their head off so they can have an excuse why they failed. I was like that, but I know I can't be like that anymore. I can't tell you exactly everything I feel, man. I don't really understand it all myself. But I have this really weird feeling that the odds are actually stacked *in* my favor.

"This music thing has been stuck in my head like a sinus infection for about five years. I'm here in Nashville to find out once and for all exactly what it's all about. To see if God's just playing a big joke on me or if He wants me to knock the country music world on its ear."

Garth sat back down.

"I don't know what to say, Garth, except that I think you

and Stephanie are going to have a lot to talk about. Now I think I'm gonna go to bed. It's after midnight. I'm not a young kid like you anymore."

"You sure you don't want to walk over to Music Row and show me around a little, let me get a feel for the place?"

"Not tonight. We'll go look around tomorrow before we hook up with Stephanie."

"Well, then I think I'm going to go ahead and walk over there."

"Suit yourself. But be careful. There's a lot of shady characters in this town."

"That's exactly what my mom told me."

Bob got up the next morning and was relieved to find Garth had made it back from his solo excursion into the night. He was snoring on the couch, a half-filled glass of watery Coke next to him on the coffee table. Jed was still fast asleep. After the two new Nashvillians got up, they showered, had coffee, and started going through the paper to look for available houses to rent. Bob again was tempted to ask Garth where he had gone the night before, but refrained. He decided that it was best not to get too nosy with someone he didn't really know, especially someone so unusually intense. But during the week and a half under Bob's roof, Garth gave Bob plenty of other reasons to be curious. Garth began receiving a lot of phone calls from people he never volunteered to identify. And when Bob and Jed went out to hit the town at night, Garth usually begged off, staying in the apartment to write songs or play his guitar. But one day while Jed was gone, Garth hinted to Bob that someone, presumably someone with money, had offered to help him if he could make some headway on his own, make certain connections, and play a certain

number of showcases. Bob didn't pry into who the anony-
mous sugar-daddy or -mama might be, but suspected it
was somebody from Oklahoma. Every time he and Garth
spoke, Bob grew more and more impressed with what this
starry-eyed twenty-five-year-old had going for him. Or
seemed to.

The one evening Garth accompanied Bob and Jed out
on the town proved to be fateful. Stephanie asked the three
to meet her at a club on Second Avenue called Windows
on the Cumberland.

"Nashville treating you all right so far, Garth?" asked
Stephanie.

"Yes ma'am," said Garth.

"You sure are formal, Mr. Brooks."

"Around the ladies especially, ma'am," said Garth.

"Well, I think that's nice. A delicate Southern belle like
me appreciates manners, y'all."

Everyone laughed. Bob and Jed ordered drinks. Stephanie and Garth ordered Cokes.

"Garth, you don't drink?" asked Stephanie.

"No, ma'am."

"You don't drink, you don't smoke. What *do* you do?"

"Garth mainlines sugar," said Jed.

"But I'm trying to cut back," deadpanned Garth. "So
now I'm shootin' saccharine."

"Oh, I see. You guys are really out here to try out for
Hee Haw," Stephanie laughed. She then quickly got down
to business. "Look, Garth, like Bob probably already told
you, I own two music publishing companies. I came to this
town thinking I was gonna set the world on fire with my
songs, but I kind of graduated into the publishing business.
We do demos in the studio, then turn around and pitch

177

'em to the record companies. I have a few producers I work with regularly. We're always looking for new singers and new material."

"I'm definitely interested," Garth said, then shot a glance at Jed. "*We're* interested."

"I'd like to hear Garth do 'Luck of the Draw,'" suggested Bob, looking at Stephanie.

"What's that?" asked Garth.

"A tune Greg Jacobs and I wrote. It's about trying to make it in Nashville. Stephanie's company's trying to sell it."

"That's a good idea," said Stephanie. "Might be right up your alley, Garth."

Stephanie suddenly stood up and got her purse. "Let's get after it."

178

"Tonight?" asked Garth. "Now?"

"Sure," said Stephanie. "What're we waitin' for?"

The four left the club and drove to Stephanie's apartment. It was around midnight. When they arrived, Stephanie dug around in a briefcase and came out with the lyrics to "Luck of the Draw." She handed the lyric sheet to Garth and her guitar to Bob.

"Play it for him, Bob," said Stephanie. She began hooking up her four-track cassette recorder and setting up a microphone for Garth. Bob sang and played the song while Garth listened and watched Bob's hands, memorizing the chord pattern in the time it took to play.

"Good tune, good lyrics," said Garth, nodding his head after Bob finished. "Let's see that guitar for a second." Garth ran through the song, quickly assimilating the lyrics and chords in his head, but giving the melody a different twist.

"OK if I sing it like that, Bob?" asked Garth. "It feels better that way."

Bob shrugged his shoulders. "Knock yourself out."

"You ready?" Stephanie asked.

"Ready as I'll ever be," said Garth, a little perplexed by the series of events that led to his being in a strange woman's apartment recording music at one in the morning. His one link to reality, Jed, was sitting on Stephanie's living room couch, silently smoking, watching the proceedings without expression. Garth adjusted his headphones, cleared his throat, and concentrated on the lyrics. "Go ahead."

Stephanie rolled the tape and Garth started strumming. In the middle of the first verse, his voice broke. "Sorry. Let's start over."

"It's OK, Garth," said Stephanie. "Just relax. I can already tell you've got a hell of a voice. Just sing it like you know how."

They got all the way through the song on the next take. Stephanie make some melody suggestions and they recorded three more takes.

"OK, Garth," said Stephanie. "I'm getting pretty tired now. Let's do one more and then I've got to go to bed. This time I want you to do it with *feeling*. Know what I mean?"

"Feeling," Garth repeated. "All right. You got it. I'm gonna nail it this time."

Stephanie punched the record button and Garth started picking.

There's a difference between winners and losers
That decides who'll fly and who'll fall.

179

It's a fact, it's a factor,
But if you're a good enough actor
You'll come out all right after all;
It ain't all in the luck of the draw.

The next day, Jed and Garth got up early and drove around town looking for a place to sleep five musicians, two wives, one small boy, Jed's cat Kit, and the Brooks's Siberian Husky, Sasha. All of the houses within the city limits were either too expensive, too small, or both. For their last house inspection of the day, they drove out to the Nashville suburb Hendersonville to check out an old five-bedroom, three-bath house. It was certainly large enough, which was the main priority, and not too shabby compared to most of the places in Stillwater. They decided that if they couldn't find anything better in the next couple of days, they'd take it, even if it was a bit removed from where all the action was.

Stephanie had gotten up early that day, too, to go to Alabama for business. While driving back, she listened with fresh ears to the cassette tape they'd recorded the night before.

"Oh, my God!" she said. The minute she walked into her apartment she called Bob Childers.

"Bob, get that kid on the phone."

"Hey, Garth, you got a phone call." This time it was from someone Bob knew. Garth grabbed the receiver.

"This is Stephanie. Garth, I was driving around today and I listened to your tape about fifty times. I'm just gonna say it plain and simple, kid. You're the best I ever heard.

The *best*."

Garth laughed. "C'mon, you're puttin' me on."

"Look, I know we just met last night and you don't know me from Eve. But there's something about you and there's something about your voice that blows me away. I want to use you in some demos. And I also want some other people to hear this tape. That OK with you?"

Garth was shaking his head in disbelief. "Yes, ma'am." He hung up the phone and sat down.

"What was that all about?" asked Bob.

"Oh, nothing, really. Stephanie was saying how much she likes your song."

After two more days of searching, Jed and Garth decided to rent the house in Hendersonville. They signed a six-month lease and then promptly told the rest of the gang in Stillwater to pack their bags. The following week, Garth and Jed loaded their gear into Jed's truck.

"Bob, I can't thank you enough for puttin' up with us this week," said Garth.

"It was my pleasure, boys," said Bob. "It sure livened my life up a little bit. Enjoyed gettin' to know you, Garth. Hope you can stick it out here awhile."

"We'll do our damnedest. Sandy'll be out today, so we're just gonna set up the house and then get the band in here and start doin' the showcases. Oh, and here you go." Garth handed Bob an envelope with a wad of money.

"I said you guys didn't have to pay me, man," Bob said.

"A deal's a deal. That's for the rent and the phone. And any damage Jed may have done," Garth said. "Home, Jed."

Sandy arrived in Hendersonville later that evening, with the Brooks's dog and the rest of their possessions in tow. Garth, Sandy, and Jed immediately set about arranging

181

the furniture and sprucing things up. It was an exciting time, the three of them working together day and night preparing for the rest of the Santa Fe family to move in. A few nights before the rest of the band was to head for Tennessee, Tom called Jed.

"So, Jed, what's the place like?" asked Tom, sounding nervous.

"Pretty nice, really," assured Jed. "Sandy's giving it the woman's touch."

"It's a dump, isn't it? Man, I don't know about this. I can't move my kid into some fleabag joint." Tom was getting cold feet, understandably concerned for his young son in a house full of struggling musicians. His last trip to Nashville, the previous December, had left a bad taste in his mouth. He had gone out to be on the "You Can Be a Star" program, a "Gong Show" type format in which judges—typically performers past their prime and/or Nashville brass—awarded scores after each performance and chose a winner at the end of the show. It was a nerve-wracking experience. Tom performed a song he had written, "She Gave Away Her Heart," only to be given what he considered an unfairly low score by one of the judges, a man he called "one of them music-industry necktie types."

182

Tom eventually got over his jitters, and the rest of the band and significant others soon joined Jed and Garth. Immediately they went to work practicing original songs, which excited everyone. After all, they had come here to be an original music band. The dance scene was behind them. They'd make it on their own merits or they wouldn't make it at all.

In order to work toward landing some paying gigs,

they lined up a couple of showcases: exposure-only venues where agents from record labels are known to hang out, searching for talent. Because they didn't expect any money from playing anytime soon, they went out and found real jobs. In order to take care of Jeremy, the Skinners needed to alternate their work schedules, so Tom took a night job at a convenience store he called the "Stop 'n Rob," and Jeri took a day job as a cashier at a local Wal-Mart. Mike got work as a peon in an office furniture warehouse, breaking his back loading chairs into boxes during the graveyard shift. Troy landed a maintenance job at an apartment complex. Jed left the house every morning and showed up in the evening but no one knew what he was doing. And Garth, who was finding a little more luck than when he first visited Nashville, got the cushiest job of all, as a boot-shop manager, thanks in part to his DuPree Sports experience. By a stroke of unbelievable luck, or through some clever persuasion by Garth, Sandy got hired on at the same store. So with paying the rent not the worry it can be for many struggling musicians in an expensive town like Nashville, they started doing what they'd set out to do.

Their first showcase was at the Nashborough Palace. Instead of playing before a horde of industry brass starved for fresh talent, like they'd hoped, they spent the night serenading a bunch of drunks thirsty for another shot. After playing a nervous set of originals and receiving a less than lukewarm response, Garth decided they should revert to playing covers in the second set. The crowd perked up a little when it began to recognize some of the songs, but the band knew it didn't mean as much to be playing other people's material, stuff that every other band in Nashville played. During a break, Garth made a suggestion.

"Maybe we all should dress more, you know, appropriately," he said, pointing with his eyes at Tom's and Mike's tennis shoes, Jed's black T-shirt and Troy's old flannel shirt. The others looked at Garth's tight Wranglers and cowboy hat and boots. "I mean, this is Nashville. We should look the part." No one said anything. "I know a place where you can get some boots," he laughed, trying to slice through the sudden tension. He wasn't implying that they should dress like the Texas Playboys, but his message was clear.

"Yeah, maybe you got a point," Tom muttered. Tom was not thrilled at having just played a set of covers, but he kept his characteristic cool. Wearing cowboy gear, he thought, wasn't the answer to their problems.

184   But it was only their first showcase, and they ended up playing two others at the Nashborough Palace. Garth and Tom, perhaps subconsciously sensing that the end was nigh, began looking for other showcases and writers' nights to play when the band wasn't doing anything.

Around the house, tension gradually began to mount. The band's creative differences, too complex to be fully articulated, were manifested in irrational, isolationist behavior. When they first settled into the house, they typically ate dinner together in the kitchen. All of a sudden meals were being eaten in the solitude of bedrooms. Mike and Garth began to pass in the hallways without acknowledging each other. Doors slammed without explanation. Tempers flared when someone stayed in the bathroom too long. A Jeremy coughing fit that woke half the house sent cranky people to work the next day. Dog and cat fur produced sneezing and bad moods. Jed and

Troy were too loud when they came in late at night. Jeri fumed at the unknown person who kept drinking all the orange juice. Personal space and time alone became the most precious commodities in the world. It was the normal series of communication breakdowns among roommates. But these were roommates whose amiable cohabitation depended upon maintaining a common purpose, one that had uprooted them all from relative comfort and stability. And that purpose was rapidly unraveling.

The end finally came at Nashville's Sutler Inn. The band was on the same showcase bill as Dobie "Gimme the Beat, Boys" Gray. After opening with a few originals that produced a lackluster response from the audience, a tense Garth decided not to wait for the end of the set to whip out the covers.

"Let's do 'Honky Tonk Man,'" he blurted out. Tom and Jed looked at each other. Mike and Troy turned their heads and pretended they hadn't heard. Garth looked out at the audience. "Here's one I know'll get you going. It's one by our old friend Dwight Yoakam."

It was the right call. The crowd perked up. Hey, these guys can really play, they thought. That guy can sing, that guitarist can wail, that blonde dude can fiddle, that drummer can thump, and that bassist can harmonize like Phil Everly. These boys do Dwight Yoakam proud, they enthusiastically agreed.

Santa Fe had won the battle but lost the war.

That night, Tom and Garth sat down in the kitchen. Jeri, Sandy, and Jeremy were in bed, Mike went to work at the furniture warehouse, and Jed and Troy slipped over to Bob Childers's apartment to escape the bad vibes at Santa Fe Manor. Tom poured himself a cup of coffee and lit a

185

cigarette. Garth poured a Coke.

"Garth, I don't think I can do this anymore."

Garth didn't flinch. He seemed prepared for Tom's statement. "Look, man, I know things haven't been great, but we've gotta stick this thing out. It sounds corny and probably not what you want to hear right now, but you just gotta have faith."

"I gotta have more than that, Garth. What I know is what I see. And you and I—all of us, I think—aren't seein' eye to eye on what this band's about. I thought we were here to be a group."

"We *are* a group."

"Yeah, but we're not a group doing our own thing. We keep going back to the same stuff we did in Stillwater. That's not what I'm here for. This band's going nowhere fast."

Garth sighed and dropped his head. All was silent. Then he looked at Tom.

"Look, I know this might sound weird, but what would you say if I could *guarantee* we're gonna make it?"

Tom looked puzzled, then chuckled. "I'd say how in the hell are you gonna do that?"

"I can't tell you—yet. You just gotta trust me. All I can tell you is that I *know* this band's gonna make it."

Without something more tangible than Garth's nebulous guarantee to keep him interested, Tom decided to go ahead and announce he was quitting. Mike took Tom's lead and quickly followed suit. With Tom and Mike gone, there really wasn't a band left for Jed and Troy to quit. Suddenly the ex-members of Santa Fe, five sets of dreams that were once united, were setting their sights not on stardom but on one eagerly anticipated day four months

And then there was one. Photo credit: *Stillwater NewsPress.*

away, when the lease on the house expired and they could   187
get away from one another.

On the positive side, though, the pressure was off. Each person could set about doing what he or she wanted to do. And, just like that, good things began to happen. Tom landed a rather enviable job repairing and inspecting Gibson guitars at the company's Nashville plant, working alongside another frustrated musician named Joe Diffie. Soon after, Jed got a job there, too, and made some extra income by joining a band with Troy. Mike continued to toil thanklessly in the warehouse all night long, but at least he wasn't having to do so after playing to indifferent audiences. And Garth, with Sandy covering for him at the boot store, found more time for writing songs in the back room.

On a cool October evening, Tom and Garth were playing the same showcase at a club called the Bluebird

Café. Among others on the bill was Joe Diffie. While someone else was playing onstage, Tom introduced Garth to Joe. Tom and Garth were getting along much better since they'd begun pursuing their own careers. While the three were talking, Garth noticed somebody waving to him.

"Excuse me a second, guys. I see someone back there I know." He walked to the back of the club and sat down with two gentlemen in business suits. Joe and Tom sat down at a table to talk about that day's work at Gibson and philosophize about making it in the business. Half an hour later, Garth came back and joined Tom and Joe.

"Who're those guys back there, Garth?" asked Tom. "The mafia?"

"Yeah," Garth laughed. "They want me to rub some-one out. Actually, that one dude there on the right is Bob Doyle."

"I've heard of him," said Joe. "He's with ASCAP, ain't he?"

"Yeah, he is," replied Garth, his mouth forming an odd grin. "For the time being."

Garth looked over at Tom and started to say something, but Tom was busy watching the nervous performer on-stage, feeling empathy for him. The singer was stumbling through his song, playing wrong chords and humming his way through forgotten lyrics. Had he been playing in a regular bar, no one in the audience would have noticed. But at a songwriters' showcase in Nashville, everyone did, and he knew it. And as if his awkward performance wasn't unsettling enough, a large bead of nervous sweat raced down the middle of his forehead to the tip of his nose and remained there, defying gravity. He tried jerking his head to knock it off, but it wouldn't budge. Finally he leaned forward and scraped it off with the microphone. The audience rolled their eyes in disgust. The singer finished his set, mercifully, and Tom was up next.

"If I don't play any better than the last guy, shoot me," Tom said to Garth as he walked toward the stage.

"You'll do great, man," said Garth. "Just don't put your lips on that mike."

Tom introduced himself and started his set. "Tom's got one hell of a sweet voice, doesn't he, Garth?" Joe whispered. Garth nodded but he was miles away, staring right through Joe, through Tom, through the wall of the Bluebird Café, and through the ozone layer. Garth took a swig of his Coke and released a sigh that blew his bar napkin to the floor.

Then, suddenly, all hell broke loose.

189

Epilogue

"There was one incident that convinced me Garth was going to make it," said Bob Childers, looking back on his days in Nashville. "It was a couple months after the band broke up. We were at Sixteenth Avenue Studio. Garth was doing a demo of 'Luck of the Draw,' a song he wrote called 'Mr. Right Tonight,' and some other tune I can't remember. He was in the middle of singing when the producer stopped everything and suggested that Garth sing a line differently.

"Now, most singers I know are pretty stubborn. Most guys would've held their ground and told the producer to shove it. It's what I probably would've done, and I could tell that's what Garth felt like saying. But then he just nodded his head and said, 'You're right. You're the producer and I'm the singer,' and then sang the line exactly like the producer wanted.

"That told me all I needed to know."

Stephanie Brown needed nothing but Garth's voice to convince her of his potential. After she presented Garth's demo tape to her friend Bob Doyle, the ASCAP executive got to know the young singer and immediately recognized that there was something special about him. Doyle decided to leave ASCAP to start his own music publishing business. His first client was, of course, Garth, whom he signed in November 1987. Doyle then formed a partnership with Pam Lewis and signed Garth to a management contract in January 1988. Only three months later, less than ten months after Santa Fe had moved to Nashville, Garth signed a record deal with Capitol.

How likely is it for a complete unknown to land a major record contract that fast in Music City, USA? About as likely as hitting the jackpot on the first try on every slot machine in Las Vegas. Because of the sheer lightning speed of Garth's rise to the top, it's hard to believe that he didn't know somebody with serious Nashville leverage before he moved out there. That would help explain the mysterious phone calls at Bob Childers's apartment, his meetings with unidentified people, and his pleading and fuzzy guarantee to Tom the night the band broke up, among other things. But even if Garth knew every entertainment executive in America from the time he was in kindergarten, that would still not explain how he, at the age of only thirty-four, had already sold more albums than anyone in history except the Beatles. No person or group of people can arrange that kind of success. A combination of so many things—talent, passion, intelligence, timing, luck, genes, and determination—made it all possible. Garth's unique ability to straddle the country and pop music worlds hasn't hurt either.

Epilogue

True to his word, though, Garth didn't forget about the little people. His contract with Capitol allowed him to assemble the touring band he wanted, enabling him to keep the promise he had made to his friends years earlier back at Iba Hall in Stillwater. He first called Ty England, who seized the opportunity by the jugular and became Garth's touring rhythm guitarist and backup singer. Ty later would use the experience with Garth to start his own successful career as a solo artist.

Then Garth called Dale Pierce. Under any other circumstances, Dale would have hung up the phone before Garth even finished asking the question, sprinted to his truck, and hightailed it to Nashville. But at the time, Dale's heart was being stretched every which way. He had gotten married a few months earlier, only to have the blessed event dampened the same week by the death of his father. To make matters more complicated, he had just found out that his wife was pregnant. So instead of hopping on the Garth Brooks gravy train, Dale remained in Stillwater to bring his son into the world. To support his young family, he started a carpet-cleaning business.

Jed and Troy were the only Santa Fe members who kept in contact with Garth immediately after the band parted ways. Jed sat in on a few showcases and demo recordings when Garth needed a guitarist. When the Capitol deal was signed, Garth asked Jed to join the touring group. But Jed, having played with Mel McDaniel in the early 1980s, had learned a little bit about the music business and knew that touring musicians often got the short end of the stick when supporting big names. Certain that Garth was going to be a big star, Jed agreed to tour as long as he could also play on the albums, get his name established, build a career. Besides, he thought it was only fair since he'd been with Garth back in the days of Bink's and Honky-Tonk Hell. But in Nashville, road bands and studio musicians rarely penetrate each other's sphere. That's simply the Nashville way. Garth, his hands tied, couldn't make any such promise, so Jed said no dice.

Garth also asked Troy to play, but like Dale he was in the midst of several personal crises. Back in Oklahoma, Troy's father was dying, so he was traveling back and forth to visit whenever he could. His apartment-maintenance job barely afforded the frequent trips, and soon he fell behind on his bills and child-support payments. Gibson, the company that for some reason was so friendly to ex–Santa Fe members, came to the rescue by offering Troy a job that pulled him out of the financial hole. When Garth called to offer him the drummer position, Troy decided that he couldn't risk abandoning the security of ample, steady money and benefits. He and Jed lived for several years in a house in the suburb of Hermitage until Troy could afford to get his own place in Nashville. Both continued to work at Gibson and play in bands.

Tom hung around Nashville for two more years until he decided that the big city really wasn't the atmosphere to rear young Jeremy, so he and Jeri moved back to the familiar soil of Bristow, to a little place in the country where Tom felt most at home. Jeri's career with the Mervyn's department store chain took the Skinner family to Baton Rouge, Louisiana, where Tom explored a new musical universe called Zydeco. The family later moved back to the Tulsa area. Tom's songwriting career began to take off in 1995 when a tune he co-wrote with Bob Wiles, "Used to Be," was recorded by Wiles's Oklahoma band the Red

Epilogue

Dirt Rangers—which at one time included Dale Pierce—
and was featured on a tribute album to Route 66, "Songs
from the All-American Highway," which received national
airplay and critical acclaim. In 1996, Tom recorded and
released his first album, on the Binky Records label (no
relation to Bink) in Baton Rouge. Brothers Mike and
Craig both played and sang on the album. Mike stayed
in Nashville a little longer than Tom, but he also decided
to return to his hometown. He took a job as a driver for
a national distributor of gourmet foods, and continued to
fiddle around in bands.

I have a particular memory of Garth that is engraved
forever in my mind, one of those memories that can be recalled as clearly as the moment it happened, like when my
children were born or the time I met Buddy Rich in Stillwater. In early 1989, I was walking down Cherry Street in
Tulsa on my way to get a paper. I passed by a record store
called Sound Warehouse and glanced inside. In the dis-
play windows were five big Garth posters staring back at
me: promotion for his debut album. I stopped and looked
at my old bandmate. "Hey, Garth," I said out loud, momentarily caught up in the illusion that he was really there.
Inside the store was a group of tough-looking teenagers
checking out the rap albums and jiving around. "Garth," I
said, gazing deeply into his airbrushed mug, "what in the
hell are you doing in *there*?"

But now I know. So does the rest of humanity. Garth
belongs wherever the music is, because he's responsible
for one of the most exciting periods in country music

Bob Childers, Austin, Texas, 1989. Bob was responsible for introduc-
ing Garth to Stephanie Brown, who introduced Garth to Bob Doyle,
who introduced Garth to superstardom. Photo by Terry Balch.

history. He's the leader of America's Band, just like he said
he would be. He persevered, got lucky as hell, and now
he's living the fantasy of every person who ever plucked a
guitar or belted out a tune in the shower.

The last time I actually spoke to Garth was in the fall
of 1988. Through the grapevine I heard he was coming to
Tulsa to play an annual benefit for the Brush Creek Boys

Ranch, an organization for troubled teens. He had performed at this event for years, and he and Sandy weren't
about to miss it. I decided to go see what the old bumpkin
was up to.

The event was held at a country crafts fair in suburban
south Tulsa. Little girls were running around in flowery
dresses with ribbons in their hair, little cowboys chasing
after them. In a barn-turned-bazaar, ladies in gingham
dresses stood by tables and tables of pottery, wreaths
made out of sticks, handmade dolls, potpourri, and weird
things inside pickling jars—a multitude of rustic accents
for the home. Outside, older gentlemen sporting straw
hats and big sideburns were broiling animal flesh in gigantic Hasty-Bake ovens. The aroma of well-done meat
competed mightily with that of hay and manure. Down
the slope from the barn, an old, rickety trailer bed had
been wheeled out next to a decaying rail fence to serve
as a stage. Long tables and chairs were set up so that everyone could sit and munch burgers and potato salad and
bake in the sun and knock over one another's lemonade
while swatting at all the gnats and big green flies. Country
fellowship at its finest.

I sat down by Garth's old pal and writing partner, Randy
Taylor, whom I hadn't seen since I'd left Stillwater. We ate
and joked about the old days at Bink's. Randy was a Bink's
regular, and he was one of the few cowboys I ever got to
know very well. Pretty soon, Garth's GMC Jimmy pulled
up and a dozen kids ran up and hugged him and patted
him on the back. It was easy to see that Garth really loved
being there; his grin was so big it nearly tore his face in
half.

Randy and I went over to the truck to help him unload

197

his little Peavey sound system, the same one he used to use at Willie's. I guess all of the little kids put Garth in a huggy mood, because when he saw me, he shot past my outstretched hand and put me in a bear hug. I was a little taken aback, not expecting such a warm reception; I'd always felt a little guilty for having abandoned the group in its prime. I think it was the first time I had ever been hugged by a man, so that added to my bewilderment. Sandy was with Garth and she also gave me a hug, which felt a little more natural.

We loaded all of his equipment on the trailer and then sat back to watch Garth do his bit. He started out with some James Taylor, did a little Jim Croce, some Fogelberg, some Merle Haggard, the same kind of show he used to do at Willie's. With all of the distractions of the vendors and the kiddie games going on, I didn't expect many people to pause to listen to a guy singing through a cheap PA. But an air of respect for Garth's performance, near reverence, was obvious. Everyone truly appreciated Garth's being there, especially the kids, who giggled and went crazy every time Garth winked or made a face at them.

After his first set, it was time for me to go and do whatever was so important to me back then, probably watching a baseball game in my parents' living room. I walked up to the stage and told Garth goodbye and good luck.

"By the way," he said, "I'll be sending you a check for sixty bucks."

"What for?"

"After the band broke up, we sold the equipment that we bought with the band fund and divvied up the money."

I didn't remember buying any band equipment. "Don't worry about it," I said. "I don't need it." A month before,

I had landed my first job in advertising, making eighteen thousand dollars a year, which to me then was a pile of money that eclipsed the sun. I never did find a teaching job.

"Well, I'm gonna send it to you anyway," he said.

"OK, Garth," I said as I waved goodbye, "do whatever you want to do."

I pulled away from country heaven thinking what a noble fellow I was to refuse money that was rightfully mine. That poor old struggling songwriter probably could use it to pay his electric bill, I thought. I wasn't aware at the time that he had signed with Capitol Records.

Garth never sent the check, and I forgot all about it until I was talking to Jed about four years later when I was digging up memories for this book. Jed said Garth had put him in charge of sending me the money, but it had just slipped his mind. I told him not to worry about it. But Jed did send me the check, and I used it to pay my electric bill.

The very last time I saw Garth was in 1989 at the Tulsa City Limits. He was touring to promote his first album, and I decided to go because my sister had become a fan of his and wanted someone to accompany her. It was my first trip to a country joint since I'd watched Santa Fe play its last gig there two years earlier. The place was stuffed, and half the crowd were Garth's old Stillwater cronies, including every single employee from DuPree Sports. Sandy was all dolled up and sashaying through the crowd, greeting everyone as if we had come to her home. It truly was a homecoming. I was talking to Sandy as Garth's act was announced. She vanished off to her VIP table and my sister and I made our way to our seats. Here came Garth, wearing the tightest blue jeans imaginable and a black shirt that looked as if it were made out of iron. Then came the drummer, the steel player, the fiddler, the rhythm guitarist, the bass player, the lead guitarist, yet another guitarist—they just kept coming and coming. Outside of a jazz swing band, I'd never seen so many musicians on one stage.

The crowd came to its feet, led by the inebriated DuPree Sports throng. Garth sauntered up to the microphone, his face a strange combination of confidence and disbelief, and screamed as loudly as he possibly could: "Hello Tulsa Oklahoma!"

Garth Brooks had landed on earth. Everyone in the crowd knew it. It was what they were waiting for, what he was waiting for. I had always been confused about why Garth was so hell-bent on making it big in the music world, how he could maintain such passion for one thing. But that moment when he walked onstage clarified everything.

They ripped into "Nobody Gets Off in This Town." The band was beyond tight; it was squeaky clean, abnormally meticulous, musicians working together in perfect precision. Naturally I began comparing Santa Fe with Garth's new band, Stillwater, but the contrasts far outweighed the similarities. Santa Fe was good, but we were more like Neil Young's Crazy Horse—much more raucous, mostly due to Jed's screeching guitar and my cymbal-heavy drumming. But I noticed that Garth hadn't completely exorcised Santa Fe from his performing persona. He, out of all those people onstage, brandished a conspicuously rough edge.

The crowd never left Garth. All the tight-jeaned women and big, beefy cowboys were moving their lips to every song, and there was simply no way to stuff any more bodies on the dance floor. Then, in tribute to the DuPree

200

Sports gang and others who had driven all the way in from Stillwater, Garth excused his band and closed the show by singing "American Pie," the song he often sang at Willie's to wrap up the evening, accompanied only by his guitar. The crowd gave him a thunderous ovation, and as soon as the applause ended people swarmed to the stage for autographs, which he signed until two in the morning.

I almost got in line, to congratulate him on a great show and let him know I came. I sensed that it would probably be one of the last times I'd get to talk to him in person, because it was obvious that he was going to be more popular than even he would ever have dared imagine. Just looking at the mass of cowboy hats gathered around him told me all I needed to know about his destiny. He was going to be famous, for sure, but only the most insane mind could have predicted the magnitude of his fame.

Garth and I were friends, but we were never close pals. We spent a lot of time playing music together, but I never dropped over to his house to watch a ball game or anything. We had many laughs together. Santa Fe was unquestionably the funniest group of people I ever played music with. That and the money were the two reasons I stayed in the group as long as I did.

But just as Garth had insight into his destiny, so did I into mine, and our lives were never meant to intersect except for one brief period in a little college town in Oklahoma. Sometimes I wish I could go back to that time, only because it was so much simpler, without the pressure of supporting a family, enduring insensitive bosses, trying to stay sane with a measly two weeks of vacation per year, worrying about my diet, and all of the daily concerns of the American proletarian. Garth, I'm sure, relishes that period, too. But times have dramatically changed. While I will always be able to enjoy the freedom simply to go for a walk in my neighborhood or drive to the store whenever we're running low on milk or bananas, Garth will never again lead a normal life. Having gorged on the fruits of his labor, he will forevermore experience the spoils and the heartache, the glory and the isolation, the double-edged sword of immense fame.

I have a strange feeling I'll meet him again someday, though it's hard to imagine where or why. After all he's seen and done since we parted ways, he'll probably struggle to remember how he knows me. But when it all comes back to him, so will the memories of a much simpler time. Then he'll smile and give me a hug, and I'll hug him back, and it won't feel unnatural at all. We'll talk, have a few laughs, brag about our kids, then return to our respective realities, both of us deeply thankful that we've found our destiny.

Photo credit: *Stillwater NewsPress.*